LATER SCOTS-IRISH LINKS 1725–1825

by David Dobson

CLEARFIELD

Printed for
Clearfield Company, Inc. by
Genealogical Publishing Co., Inc.
Baltimore, Maryland
2003

International Standard Book Number: 0-8063-5215-9

Made in the United States of America

LATER SCOTS-IRISH LINKS, 1725-1825

The emphasis of Scottish emigration during the seventeenth century was to Ulster, during which period nearly 100,000 Scots settled in the northern province of Ireland. This situation changed dramatically during the eighteenth century when the destination of most Scots emigrants was across the Atlantic to the British colonies in North America and the West Indies. The period also witnessed the beginning of the large scale exodus from Ireland to the Americas. However, some movement of people from Scotland to Ireland did happen in the eighteenth century, but it was minimal compared to the period of the Plantation of Ulster. There was also some movement from Ireland to Scotland; much of it was of a temporary nature as young men, generally of Scottish origin, often headed for Scotland to complete their education or professional training, some of whom then followed their countrymen across the Atlantic. The substantial number of students from Ireland matriculating at Scottish universities results from the contemporary policy of English and Irish universities which restricted access to those in communion with the Church of England. This meant that Presbyterians and other religious dissenters in Ireland sent their sons to Scottish universities, especially those in Glasgow and Edinburgh. Scotland generally produced too many graduates for its domestic requirements which resulted in many of them seeking careers in the American colonies, often as physicians, schoolmasters and ministers.

This book identifies both Scots in Ireland and Irish in contemporary Scotland based mainly on primary sources in Scotland, such as university records, court records, gravestone inscriptions, family and estate papers, as well as various published sources.

David Dobson
St Andrews, Scotland. 2003.

LATER SCOTS-IRISH LINKS, 1725-1825

ABELL, RICHARD, from Ireland, graduated MD from
Edinburgh University in 1822 [GME#66]

ABERNETHY, JOHN, born near Templepatrick in 1736,
educated in Scotland, a Presbyterian minister in Ireland
1769-1802, died in Antrim 8 April 1818. [FI#VI.129]

ADAIR, Mrs ISOBEL, relict of Mr Patrick Adair, minister at
Carrickfergus, 1767. [NAS.CS16.1.130/145]

ADAIR, WILLIAM, son of James Adair, a farmer in Drumara,
County Down, matriculated at Glasgow University in
1811, graduated MA 1814. [RGG#2]

ADAMS, BENJAMIN, son of Allan Adams in Knockbride,
County Cavan, matriculated at Glasgow University in
1772, graduated BA in 1774. [RGG#4]

ADAMS, JAMES, graduated MA from Glasgow University in
1817, an Irish Presbyterian minister at Castledearg 1820-
1837, died 22 May 1837. [RGG#4]

ADAMS, JOHN, son of William Adams a merchant in
Dungiven, educated in Glasgow 1740, a Presbyterian
minister in Ireland 1745, died 8 June 1789. [FI.VI.129]

ADAMS, JOHN, born in Donaghadee, graduated MA from
Glasgow University in 1765, a Presbyterian minister at
Donaghadee 1772-1779 who died 9 January 1779.
[RGG#4][FI.VI.129]

ADAMS, JOHN ALEXANDER, graduated MA from Glasgow
University in 1813, possibly a Presbyterian minister in
Monaghan 1818-1820, Strabane 1820-1827, who died 17
December 1827. [RGG#4]

ADAMS, MATTHEW, graduated MA from Glasgow
University in 1812, a Presbyterian minister at Corlea
1824-1833. [RGG#4]

ADAMS, ROBERT, graduated MA from Glasgow University in 1803, possibly a Presbyterian minister at Clare, ordained 1807, died 1840. [RGG#5]

ADAMS, SAMUEL, from Ireland, graduated MD from Edinburgh University in 1796. [GME#27]

AGNEW, ANDREW, lieutenant of the 12th Foot, married Martha de Courcy, daughter of John, lord baron of Kinsale and Ringrone, at St Multrose, Kinsale, on 21 May 1792. [NAS.GD154.337]

AGNEW, Mrs MARTHA, widow of Andrew Agnes, in Kinsale, 1793. [NAS.GD154.683/11]

AGNEW, PATRICK, of Kilwaghter, 1704. [NAS.GD154.677/1]

AGNEW, ROBERT, from Ireland, graduated MD 1796. [RGG#6]

AITKEN, JAMES, from Ireland, graduated MA from Glasgow University in 1772. [RGG#8]

AITKEN, WILLIAM, a merchant in Larne, Ireland, 1746. [NAS.RD2.167.58]; 1750. [NAS.CS16.1.84/50]

ALEXANDER, ANDREW, born 1726, son of Jacob Alexander in Glendermott, graduated MA from Glasgow University in 1745, a Presbyterian minister at Urmey and Sion, Ireland, from 1749 to 1808, died 30 April 1808. [RGG#9][FI.VI.129]

ALEXANDER, JOSIAS, from Ireland, graduated MA from Glasgow University in 1803. [RGG#11]

ALEXANDER, SAMUEL, born near Ballywalter 1704, graduated MA from Edinburgh University in 1731, a Presbyterian minister in Ireland from 1737 to 1774, died 18 November 1787. [FI.VI.129#]

ALEXANDER, THOMAS, graduated MA from Glasgow University in 1791, possibly an Irish Presbyterian minister at Cairncastle from 1793 to 1829. [RGG#11]

ALEXANDER, WILLIAM, a merchant in Dublin, 1749. [NAS.RD3.210.260]

ALISON, FRANCIS, born 1705 in County Donegal, emigrated to America in 1735, pastor of a Presbyterian church and teacher in New London, Pennsylvania, graduated DD from Glasgow University in 1756, Professsor of Moral Philosophy at the College of Philadelphia, died there on 28 November 1799. [RGG#12]

ALLAN, ROBERT, a merchant in Belfast, 1726. [NAS.AC9/967]

ALLAN, THOMAS, Island Bridge, Ireland, 1755. [NAS.RS27.146/69]

ALLEN, ANDREW, graduated MA from Glasgow University in 1773 and LL.D. in 1795 also from there, Chancellor of the Diocese of Clogher, Vicar General, Official Principal and Commissary of the Lord Bishop of Clogher. [RGG#14]

ALLEN, CHARLES, graduated MA from Glasgow University in 1821, Classical teacher, Convoy, Taphoe, County Donegal, died 1871. [RGG#14]

ALLEN, DAVID, born 1731 son of David Allen in County Tyrone, educated at Glasgow University 1758, a Presbyterian minister in Ireland 1772-1779, died in Barnhill 9 January 1812. [FI.VI.129]

ALLEN, JAMES, son of John Allen a farmer in the parish of Templemore, County Londonderry, matriculated at Glasgow University in 1766, graduated MA in 1770. [RGG#14]

ALLEN, JOHN, graduated MA from Glasgow University in 1805, an Irish Presbyterian minister in Dunfanaghy and

Kilmacrenan from 1812 to 1829, and at Kilmacrenan from 1829. [RGG#14]

ALLEN, JOHN, younger son of Alexander Allen a farmer in the parish of Newton Hamilton, County Armagh, matriculated at Glasgow University in 1805, graduated MA in 1809. [RGG#15]

ALLEN, ROBERT, second son of John Allen, a gentleman in the parish of Ray, County Donegal, matriculated at Glasgow University in 1773, graduated MA in 1775. [RGG#15]

ALLEN, ROBERT, graduated MA from Glasgow University in 1809, Irish Presbyterian minister at Stewartstown 1814 to 1849, then Superintendent of the Connaught Mission, died 1 April 1865. [RGG#15]

ALLEN, WILLIAM OWEN, from Ireland, graduated MA from Glasgow University in 1816. [RGG#15]

ALSTON, GAVIN, a merchant in Greenock, and by 1795 a merchant in Limerick. [Process of Declarator of Marriage, 1795, Commissariat of Edinburgh]

AMBROSE, WILLIAM, son of Reverend William Ambrose, graduated MA from Edinburgh University in 1724, a Presbyterian minister 1732 to 1765, died 29 December 1765. [FI.VI.130]

ANDERSON, JOHN, third son of William Anderson a merchant in County Tyrone, matriculated at Glasgow University in 1771, graduated MA in 1777.[RGG#18]

ANDERSON, JOHN, graduated MA 1809, Presbyterian minister at Aughnacloy and Ballygawley 1812-1829, died 15 May 1829. [RGG#18]

ANDERSON, JOSEPH, graduated MA from Glasgow University in 1814, Irish Presbyterian minister at Newton Crommelin from 1826 to 1834, then emigrated to America. [RGG#19]

ANDERSON, ROBERT, second son of James Anderson, a gentleman in the parish of Maghera, County Londonderry, matriculated at Glasgow University in 1808, graduated MA in 1812. [RGG#19]

ANDERSON, THOMAS, graduated MA from Glasgow University 1781, possibly Presbyterian minister at Drumquin and Pettigo, County Tyrone, 1794-1812, died 27 December 1812. [RGG#20]

ANDREWS, HENRY, from Ireland, graduated MA from Glasgow University in 1812. [RGG#21]

ANNESLEY, CHARLES, from Ireland, graduated MD from Edinburgh University in 1803. [GME#35]

ARBUCKLE, ..., in Dublin 1798. [NAS.GD307.16.16]

ARCHER, NICHOLAS, from Ireland, graduated MD from Edinburgh University in 1785. [GME#18]

ARCHER, WILLIAM, second son of Samuel Archer in County Down, matriculated at Glasgow University 1753, graduated MA 1755. [RGG#22]

ARCHIBALD, FRANCIS, born in Scotland, licentiate of the Church of Scotland, ordained as minister of Newtonards 5 August 1777, left in August 1780. [F.7.527]

ARMOR, SAMUEL, graduated MA from Glasgow University 1807, possibly Presbyterian minister at Drumquin 1812-1844, died 10 March 1844. [RGG#22]

ARMOR, SAMUEL, graduated MA from Glasgow University in 1824, Presbyterian minister at Inch near Londonderry 1833-1853, died 11 June 1863. [RGG#22]

ARMOUR, JOHN, son of William Armour in Killcliff, County Down, matriculated at Glasgow University 1744, graduated MA in 1747, emigrated to Virginia by 4 April 1750. [RGG#22]

ARMSTRONG, ANDREW, from Ireland, graduated MD from Edinburgh University in 1800. [GME#32]

ARMSTRONG, ARCHIBALD, graduated MA from Glasgow University in 1816, a Presbyterian minister at Clougherney 1823-1849, died in September 1849. [RGG#22]

ARMSTRONG, JAMES, born ca1709 in County Down, graduated MA from Edinburgh University in 1731, a Presbyterian minister in Ireland 1739, died 23 October 1779. [FI.VI.130]

ARMSTRONG, JAMES, from Ireland, graduated MD from Edinburgh University in 1789. [GME#21]

ARMSTRONG, WILLIAM, born in County Londonderry, graduated MA from Edinburgh University in 1726, a Presbyterian minister in Ireland from 1741, died 17 May 1761. [FI.VI.130]

ARMSTRONG, WILLIAM, from Ireland, graduated MD from Edinburgh University in 1798. [GME#29]

ARMSTRONG, WILLIAM, of Kingscavel, County Cavan, residing in Edinburgh 1799. [NAS.CS29.907.28]

ARNETT, JOHN, from Ireland, graduated MA from Glasgow University in 1778. [RGG#23]

ARNOLD, HUGH, graduated C.M. from Glasgow University in 1825, Ballynahinch, County Down, died 4 January 1870. [RGG#23]

ASH, LUKE, born at Magharafelt on 18 October 1705, son of Colonel Thomas Luke, graduated MA from Edinburgh University in 1725, a Presbyterian minister in Ireland from 1731, died in August 1742. [FI.VI.130]

ATKINSON, ARTHUR, in Mullerton, Ireland, around 1774. [NAS.RS38.XIII.178]

ATKINSON, EDWARD, graduated CM from Glasgow
University in 1820, of Glenwilliam Castle, Ballingarry,
County Limerick, died 1877. [RGG#25]

ATKINSON, JAMES, a merchant in Newry, County Down,
around 1774. [NAS.RS38.XIII.178]

ATKINSON, JOHN, in Mullerton, Ireland, around 1774.
[NAS.RS38.XIII.178]

AVERELL, ADAM, son of Thomas Averell in County
Londonderry, matriculated at Glasgow University in 1752,
graduated MA 1753. [RGG#26]

BACHOP, JOHN, farmer in Orchard, County Carlow, serviced
as heir to his father John Bachop, farmer there, 2
December 1802. [NAS.S/H]

BACKAS, CHARLES, from Ireland, graduated MD from
Edinburgh University in 1763. [GME#8]

BAGOT, WALTER, from Ireland, graduated MA from
Glasgow University in 1775. [RGG#26]

BAILIE, JOHN, only son of James Bailie in St Andrews parish,
County Down, matriculated at Glasgow University in
1809, graduated MA in 1811. [RGG#27]

BAILLIE, ALEXANDER, of Meikle Dunragit, 1771.
[NAS.GD135.1649]

BAIRD, JOHN, born in Paisley, Renfrewshire, educated at
Edinburgh University, a Presbyterian minister in the Isle
of Man from 1763 to 1766, then in Dublin 1767-1777,
converted to Episcopalianism ca.1778, died in 1804.
[FI.VI.130]

BAIRD, WILLIAM, second son of John Baird in Donnagore,
County Antrim, matriculated at Glasgow University in
1809, graduated MA in 1812. [RGG#29]

BALDWIN, HERBERT, from Ireland, graduated MD from
Edinburgh University in 1803. [GME#35]

BALDWIN, WILLIAM WARREN, from Ireland, graduated MD from Edinburgh University in 1797. [GME#28]

BALL, JOSEPH, from Ireland, graduated MD from Glasgow University in 1791. [RGG#30]

BANKHEAD, CHARLES, from Ireland, graduated MD from Edinburgh University in 1790. [GME#22]

BANKHEAD, JAMES, graduated MA from Glasgow University in 1794, possibly Presbyterian minister at Dromore, County Down, from 1796, died 10 January 1824. [RGG#30]

BANKHEAD, JOHN, born near Clough, County Antrim, in 1737, graduated MA from Edinburgh University in 1760, a Presbyterian minister in Ireland from 1761, died 5 July 1833. [FI.VI.130]

BARBER, SAMUEL, born 1738, son of John Barber a farmer in Killead, graduated MA from Glasgow University in 1759, Presbyterian minister at Rathfriland, County Down, 1763-1811, imprisoned for involvement during the Irish Rebellion of 1798, died 5 September 1811. [RGG#32][FI.VI.131]

BARKER, FRANCIS, from Ireland, graduated MD from Edinburgh University in 1795. [GME#26]

BARKER, ROBERT, youngest son of Reverend Barker in County Armagh, matriculated in 1772, graduated MA from Glasgow University in 1774. [RGG#33]

BARKER, WILLIAM, son of Reverend Squire Barker in Mullaghbrack, County Armagh, matriculated at Glasgow University in 1768, graduated MA in 1770. [RGG#34]

BARLOW, EDWARD, from Ireland, graduated MD from Edinburgh University in 1803. [GME#35]

BARRY, DAVID, from Ireland, graduated MD from Edinburgh University in 1756. [GME#6]

BARRY, JOHN, from Ireland, graduated MD from Edinburgh University in 1792. [GME#23]

BARTLEY, ROBERT, a physician educated in Dublin and in Edinburgh, graduated MD, settled in Londonderry, New Hampshire, around 1790. [SA#180]

BATES, ISAAC, son of William Bates, a farmer in Artrea, County Londonderry, matriculated at Glasgow University in 1766, graduated MA in 1770. [RGG#37]

BEAMISH, CHARLES, from County Cork, matriculated at Glasgow University in 1779, graduated MA in 1782. [RGG#38]

BEAMISH, JOHN, from Ireland, graduated MD from Edinburgh University in 1796. [GME#26]

BEAMISH, JOHN, from Ireland, graduated MD from Edinburgh University in 1798. [GME#29]

BELCHER, WILLIAM, from Ireland, graduated MD from Edinburgh University in 1822. [GME#66]

BELL, Reverend ALAN, master of the Diocesan School in Down, Ireland, graduated LL.D. from Glasgow University in 1817. [RGG#40]

BELL, or MCFADZEN, ANN, in Donaghadee, testament confirmed with the Commissariat of Edinburgh, 2 July 1805. [NAS.CC8.8.136.127][NAS.CC8.11.1/340]

BELL, HENRY PEILE, from Ireland, graduated MD at Glasgow University in 1826. [RGG#40]

BELL, JOHN, a pawnbroker in Belfast, serviced as heir to his father John Bell, a brickmaker in Newton Stewart, 1 April 1807. [NAS.S/H]

BELL, THOMAS, from Ireland, graduated MD from Edinburgh University in 1783. [GME#17]

BELL, THOMAS, from Ireland, graduated Ch.B. in 1822. [RGG#41]

BELLY, JOHN, Anglo-Irish, graduated MA from Glasgow University in 1730. [RGG#42]

BENNETT, JAMES, from Ireland, graduated MD from Edinburgh University in 1779. [GME#14]

BENNETT, JOHN BARTER, from Ireland, graduated MD from Edinburgh University in 1801. [GME#33]

BESNARD, ROBERT, from Ireland, graduated MD from Edinburgh University in 1800. [GME#32]

BIGGAR, JAMES, licentiate of the Church of Scotland, ordained to Newtonards 13 April 1785, returned to Scotland in 1797. [F.7.527]

BIGGS, BENJAMIN, from Ireland, graduated MD from Edinburgh University in 1803. [GME#35]

BINDEN, CECILIA, relict of Dr Nicolas Binden, Edinburgh, and of Mountgrit, Limerick, testament confirmed with the Commissariat of Edinburgh on 18 May 1818. [NAS.CC8.8.143.319]

BINDEN, NICOLAS, from Ireland, graduated MD from Edinburgh University in 1788. [GME#21]

BIRCH, DE BURGH, graduated MD from Edinburgh University in 1821. [GME#64]

BLACK, JAMES BIRCH, graduated MA from Glasgow University in 1814, Presbyterian minister at Dromora 1816 -1823. [RGG#46]

BLACK, JANET, in Richmond, Dublin, serviced as heiress to her brother John Black of Ardmarrock, formerly in Jamaica, on 16 February 1827. [NAS.S/H]

BLACK, MARGARET relict of Dr Trail the Bishop of Down, had her testament confirmed with the Commissariat of Edinburgh on 29 March 1805. [NAS.CC8.11.1/111]

BLACK, ROBERT, born 1751, graduated MA from Glasgow University in 1772, Presbyterian minister in Dromore and in Londonderry, died in Londonderry on 4 December 1817. [RGG#47]

BLACK, SAMUEL, from Ireland, graduated MD from Edinburgh University in 1786. [GME#18]

BLACK, WILLIAM, second son of Thomas Black a wright in Drumaul, County Antrim, matriculated at Glasgow University in 1779, graduated MD in 1782. [RGG#47]

BLACKALL, EDMOND, from Ireland, graduated MD from Edinburgh University in 1749. [GME#4]

BLACKMAN, JERVISE, graduated MD from Edinburgh University in 1821. [GME#64]

BLACKWOOD, THOMAS, fourth son of John Blackwood a farmer in Auchanuncion, County Donegal, matriculated at Glasgow University in 1775, graduated MA in 1778. [RGG#48]

BLAIR, ADAM, graduated MA from Glasgow University in 1737, Presbyterian minister at Horse Leap, Birr, King's County, died in Lisburn during 1790. [RGG#49]

BLAIR, ELIZABETH, in Dublin, serviced as heiress to her grandfather David Blair, miller in Newton, on 16 April 1828. [NAS.S/H]

BLAIR, JOHN, eldest son of Reverend Adam Blair in King's County, matriculated at Glasgow University in 1771, graduated MA, MD, 1775. [RGG#50]

BLAKE, HENRY, from Ireland, graduated MD from Edinburgh University in 1780. [GME#15]

BLAKE, JOHN PETER, from Ireland, graduated MD from Edinburgh University in 1803. [GME#34]

BLAKE, ROBERT, from Ireland, graduated MD from Edinburgh University in 1798. [GME#29]

BLEST, WILLIAM C., graduated MD from Edinburgh University in 1821. [GME#64]

BLYTH, ELIZABETH, daughter of Thomas Blyth of the Caithness Legion, was baptised on 7 December 1799. [Ballymodan parish register, Co. Cork]

BOGLE, KINGSMILL, son of Joseph Bogle in the parish of Donaghmore, County Donegal, matriculated at Glasgow University in 1742, graduated MA in 1744. [RGG#52]

BOISRAGON, HENRY CHARLES, from Ireland, graduated MD from Edinburgh University in 1799. [GME#30]

BOLTON, JOHN, BA, from Ireland, graduated MD from Edinburgh University in 1792. [GME#23]

BOND, JOHN, from Ireland, graduated MD from Edinburgh University in 1751. [GME#4]

BOOKER, GEORGINA CHARLOTTE, in Dublin, testament confirmed with the Commissariat of Edinburgh, on 27 November 1815. [NAS.CC8.8.147.276]

BOUCHIER, ELIZABETH, daughter of James Bouchier of the Elgin Fencibles, was baptised on 14 June 1799. [Ballyhea parish register, Co. Cork]

BOYD, JAMES, sixth son of William Boyd of Ballycastle, a gentleman in Ramoan, County Antrim, matriculated at Glasgow University in 1769, graduated MA in 1770. [RGG#56]

BOYD, ROBERT, third son of Robert Boyd a farmer in Craigs, parish of Ahoghill, County Antrim, matriculated at Glasgow University in 1813, graduated MA in 1814. [RGG#57]

BOYLE, JOHN, third son of Reverend Adam Boyle in the parish of Tamleghtoculley, County Londonderry, matriculated at Glasgow University in 1809, graduated MA in 1817. [RGG#57]

BRANDISH, WHEATON, from Ireland, graduated MD from Edinburgh University in 1792. [GME#24]

BRANNIGAN, EDWARD, born in County Armagh during 1761, session officer of Drummore, died 6 August 1821. [Kirkmadryne gravestone, Wigtownshire]

BREAKEY, ANDREW, graduated MA from Glasgow University in 1816, Presbyterian minister at Keady from 1819 to 1831, and at Killyleagh from 1831 to 1882, died 17 November 1882. [RGG#59]

BREBERTON, EDWARD, from Ireland, graduated MD from Edinburgh University in 1778. [GME#14]

BREDIN, ALEXANDER, Fort Major of Edinburgh Castle, then in Rosemount, County Donegal, cnf 4 March 1793 Commissariat of Edinburgh

BREEN, JOHN, from Ireland, graduated MD from Edinburgh University in 1802. [GME#34]

BRIDGE, JAMES, from Ireland, graduated MA from Glasgow University in 1806. [RGG#59]

BRIDGE, JOHN, from Ireland, graduated MA from Glasgow University in 1795. [RGG#59]

BRINFIELD, WILLIAM, son of William Brinfield of the Elgin Fencibles, was baptised 14 April 1799. [Ballyhea parish register, Co. Cork]

BRODY, MICHAEL, from Ireland, graduated MD from Edinburgh University in 1822. [GME#66]

BROOKE, WILLIAM, from Ireland, graduated MD from Edinburgh University in 1789. [GME#21]

BROOKS, HUGH, graduated MA from Glasgow University in 1776, possibly the Presbyterian minister at Burt, County Donegal, from 1783 to 1839, died 13 June 1839. [RGG#61]

BROUGHTON, WILLIAM, from Ireland, graduated MD from Edinburgh University in 1755. [GME#4]

BROWN, EZEKIAL, eldest son of Daniel Brown in County Tyrone, matriculated at Glasgow University in 1758, graduated MA in 1761. [RGG#62]

BROWN, GEORGE, from Ireland, graduated MD from Edinburgh University in 1779. [GME#15]

BROWN, HUGH, master and part owner of the brigantine Recovery of Belfast, 1793. [NAS.AC7/66]

BROWN, JAMES, born 1762, graduated MA from Glasgow University in 1789, possibly the Irish Presbyterian minister at Garvagh, County Londonderry, from 1795 to 1850, died 20 May 1850. [RGG#63]

BROWN, JOHN, graduated MA from Glasgow University in 1811, Presbyterian minister at Aghadowey from 1813 to 1872, graduated DD from Edinburgh University in 1839, died 27 March 1873. [RGG#64]

BROWNE, JOHN, second son of Samuel Browne a merchant in Stranorlar, County Donegal, matriculated at Glasgow University in 1822, graduated MA in 1825. [RGG#68]

BROWNE, JOSEPH, from Ireland, graduated CM from Glasgow University in 1825. [RGG#68]

BROWNE, WILLIAM, third son of William Browne a farmer in the parish of Artrea, County Londonderry, matriculated at Glasgow University in 1813, graduated MA in 1816. [RGG#68]

BRUEN, HENRY, of Oak Park, County Carlow, testament confirmed on 8 June 1807 with the Commissariat of Edinburgh. [NAS.CC8.8.137.61]

BRUMBLE, WILLIAM, of the Elgin Fencibles, married Mary Riordan, on 26 March 1799. [Ballyhea parish register, Co. Cork]

BRYAN, DANIEL, from Ireland, graduated MD from Edinburgh University in 1782. [GME#16]

BRYANTON, THOMAS JOSEPH, from Ireland, graduated MD from Edinburgh University in 1795. [GME#26]

BRYDON, GEORGE, born in Lauderdale, educated at the University of Edinburgh, licensed and ordained as a minister by the Presbytery of Earlston, to Kirkcubbin 1778, died 6 September 1817. [F.7.527]

BRYSON, ALEXANDER, second son of John Bryson a farmer in the parish of Donnegore, County Antrim, matriculated at Glasgow University in 1809, graduated MA in 1813. [RGG#73]

BRYSON, ANDREW, graduated MA from Glasgow University in 1782, Irish Presbyterian minister at Dundalk from 1788 to 1796, died in March 1797. [RGG#73]

BRYSON, JOHN, a hosier in Dublin, serviced as heir to his father Mathew Bryson, a weaver in Glasgow, 14 October 1800. [NAS.S/H]

BUCHANAN, PATRICK, a Scots-Irishman, graduated from Edinburgh University on 22 April 1736. [CEG#206]

BUCKLEY, JOSEPH, from Ireland, graduated MD from Edinburgh University in 1822. [GME#67]

BUDD, WILLIAM, from Ireland, graduated MD from Edinburgh University in 1760. [GME#7]

BULLEN, WILLIAM, from Ireland, graduated MD from Edinburgh University in 1792. [GME#23]

BURKE, JOHN, from Ireland, graduated MD from Glasgow University in 1795. [RGG#78]

BURKE, THEOBALD EDMUND, from Ireland, graduated MD from Edinburgh University in 1794. [GME#26]

BURNE, EDWARD, serviced as heir to his mother Elizabeth Miln, wife of John Burne a linen draper in Dublin, on 5 May 1774. [NAS.S/H]

BURNSIDE, THOMAS, from Ireland, graduated MD from Edinburgh University in 1787. [GME#19]

BURROUGHS, NEWBURGH, from Ireland, graduated MA from Glasgow University in 1771. [RGG#81]

BURROWES, ARNOLD, third son of Thomas Burrowes a gentleman in Stradone, County Cavan, matriculated at Glasgow University in 1766, graduated MA in 1769. [RGG#81]

BUTLER, EDMUND, from Ireland, graduated MD from Edinburgh University in 1763. [GME#8]

BUTLER, JOHN, from Ireland, graduated MD from Glasgow University in 1783. [RGG#81]

BUTLER, SAMUEL, graduated MA from Glasgow University in 1807, Irish Presbyterian minister at Magilligan from 1814 to 1862, died 9 January 1862. [RGG#81]

BUTSON, JAMES STRANGE, eldest son of Reverend Christopher Butson, Dean of Waterford, matriculated at Glasgow University in 1800, graduated MA in 1802. [RGG#82]

BYRT, ARTHUR, a merchant in Belfast, serviced as heir to his grandfather William Arthur a merchant there, 19 November 1762. [NAS.S/H]

CALDRON, JANE, daughter of William Caldron of the Caithness Legion, was baptised on 24 November 1799.[Ballymodan parish register, Co. Cork]

CALDWELL, DAVID, third son of Isaac Caldwell a farmer in the parish of Balteagh, County Londonderry, matriculated at Glasgow University in 1807, graduated MA in 1809. [RGG#83]

CALDWELL, HUGH, seventh son of Samuel Caldwell a merchant in County Londonderry, matriculated at Glasgow University in 1759, graduated MA in 1760. [RGG#84]

CALDWELL, JAMES, graduated MA from Glasgow University in 1768, possibly the Presbyterian minister at Dundonald, Belfast, from 1772 to 1814, died in October 1814. [RGG#84]

CALDWELL, JAMES, from Ireland, graduated MD from Edinburgh University in 1787. [GME#20]

CALDWELL, JOHN, from Ireland, graduated MD from Edinburgh University in 1780. [GME#15]

CALDWELL, ROBERT, graduated MA from Glasgow University in 1769, possibly the Presbyterian minister at Macosquin from 1772 to 1781, later at Moville, County Donegal, from 1784 to 1823, died in January 1823. [RGG#84]

CALDWELL, SAMUEL, from Ireland, graduated MA in 1798 and LL.D. in 1808 from Glasgow University. [RGG#84]

CALLANAN, JAMES, from Ireland, graduated MD from Edinburgh University in 1795. [GME#26]

CAMPBELL, ANNE, ninth child of John Campbell of Mamore and his wife Elizabeth Elphinstone, married Archibald Edmonstone of Duntreath in 1716, and died in Ireland on 2 November 1785. [SP.I.382]

CAMPBELL, ISABELLA, tenth child of John Campbell of Mamore and his wife Elizabeth Elphinstone, married Captain William Montgomery of Rosemount, and died in Clarendon Street, Dublin, on 3 January 1786. [SP.I.382]

CAMPBELL, Sir JAMES, of Myrreroe, County Tyrone, 1774.
[NAS.CS16.1.161/83]

CAMPBELL, JOHN, in Dublin, 1796. [NAS.GD13.239]

CAMPBELL, JOHN, from Ireland, graduated MD from
Glasgow University in 1796. [RGG#92]

CAMPBELL, JOHN, from Ireland, graduated C.M. from
Glasgow University in 1821. [RGG#92]

CAMPBELL, JOHN, in Cork, 1803. [NAS.GD13.379]

CAMPBELL, RICHARD, Scots Irish, graduated MA from
Glasgow University in 1737. [RGG#94]

CAMPBELL, WILLIAM, graduated MA from Glasgow
University in 1810, either an Irish Presbyterian minister at
Clough, County Down, from 1813 to 1829, who died in
April 1829, or an Irish Presbyterian minister at Ballymena
from 1819 to 1872, who died 26 January 1872. [RGG#85]

CARFRAE, JOHN, in Cork, 1795. [NAS.GD13.222]

CARLEY, JAMES, eldest son of John Carley a farmer in the
parish of Templecorran, County Antrim, matriculated at
Glasgow University in 1804, graduated MA in 1807.
[RGG#97]

CARLILE, FRANCIS, from Ireland, graduated MA from
Glasgow University in 1788. [RGG#97]

CARMICHAEL, WILLIAM, born in 1702, second son of
James Carmichael, Earl of Hyndford, and Elizabeth
Maitland, was consecrated Bishop of Clonfert and
Kilmacduagh in 1753, to Leighlin and Ferns in 1758, also
to Meath that year, finally Archbishop of Dublin in June
1765, he died on 15 December 1765. [SP.IV.594]

CARSON, HENRY, born 1795, graduated MA from Glasgow
University in 1809, Presbyterian minister at Glendermot,

Londonderry, from 1815 to 1870, died 3 January 1870.
[RGG#101]

CARSON, JOHN, graduated MA from Glasgow University in
1816, Irish Presbyterian minister at Templepatrick from
1831 to 1859, died 5 August 1859. [RGG#101]

CARTAN, THOMAS, from Ireland, graduated MD from
Glasgow University in 1818. [RGG#102]

CARTER, BARTHOLEMEW, from Ireland, graduated MD
from Edinburgh University in 1796. [GME#27]

CAREY, JOSEPH KNIGHT, from Ireland, graduated MD
from Edinburgh University in 1800. [GME#31]

CASEMENT, HUGH, from Ireland, graduated MD from
Edinburgh University in 1786. [GME#19]

CATHCART, THOMAS, second son of Samuel Cathcart a
farmer in the parish of Ahoghill, County Antrim,
matriculated at Glasgow University in 1796, graduated
MA in 1800. [RGG#103]

CATHCART, WILLIAM, third son of Samuel Cathcart a
farmer in the parish of Dessartmarting, County
Londonderry, matriculated at Glasgow University in 1768,
graduated MA in 1770. [RGG#103]

CAUGHTON, ROBERT, from Ireland, graduated MA from
Glasgow University in 1815. [RGG#103]

CAVANAGH, FRANCIS, from Ireland, graduated MD from
Glasgow University in 1809. [RGG#103]

CAVIN, WILLIAM, graduated MA from Glasgow University
in 1813, in Coleraine, graduated MD from Edinburgh
University in 1830. [RGG#103]

CHADWICK, RICHARD, fourth son of Richard Chadwick a
gentleman in County Tipperary, matriculated at Glasgow
University in 1771, graduated MA in 1772. [RGG#103]

CHAMBERS, JAMES, second son of William Chambers a
farmer in the parish of Dumford, County Down,
matriculated at Glasgow University in 1779, graduated
MA in 1783. [RGG#104]

CHARLES, RICHARD, eldest son of John Charles in Omagh,
County Tyrone, matriculated at Glasgow University in
1819, graduated C.M. in 1820. [RGG#105]

CHISHOLM, GEORGE, from Ireland, graduated from
Edinburgh University on 4 February 1732. [CEG#204]

CHRISTY, GEORGE, from Ireland, graduated from the
University of Edinburgh on 25 April 1734. [CEG#205]

CLAMPET, GEORGE, M.A., from Ireland, graduated MD
from Edinburgh University in 1751. [GME#5]

CLANNY, WILLIAM REID, from Ireland, graduated MD
from Edinburgh University in 1803. [GME#34]

CLARK, ISRAEL, son of John Clark a merchant in Belfast,
County Down, matriculated at Glasgow University in
1779, graduated MA in 1782. [RGG#108]

CLARK, ROBERT, third son of Robert Clark jr. a farmer in
the parish of Killeronaghan, County Londonderry,
matriculated at Glasgow University in 1812, graduated
MA in 1815. [RGG#109]

CLARKE, JOHN, in Dublin 1767. [NAS.GD124.2.307]

CLARKE, JOSEPH, from Ireland, graduated MD from
Edinburgh University in 1779. [GME#15]

CLENDINNING, JOHN, from Ireland, graduated MD from
Edinburgh University in 1790. [GME#22]

CLENDINNING, JOHN, from Ireland, graduated MD from
Edinburgh University in 1822. [GME#66]

CLERKE, JONATHAN, from Ireland, graduated MD from
Edinburgh University in 1784. [GME#17]

CLERKE, ST JOHN, from Ireland, graduated MD from
Glasgow University in 1799. [RGG#112]

CLEWLOW, JAMES, eldest son of Reverend James Clewlow
rector of a church in Bangor, County Down, matriculated
at Glasgow University in 1778, graduated MA in 1779.
[RGG#112]

COCHRAN, BERNARD, from Ireland, matriculated at
Glasgow University in 1729, graduated MA in 1730.
[RGG#113]

COCHRAN, JAMES, eldest son of James Cochran in County
Londonderry, matriculated at Glasgow University in 1763,
graduated MA in 1764. [RGG#113]

COCHRAN, ROBERT, second son of James Cochran a farmer
in County Londonderry, matriculated at Glasgow
University in 1761, graduated MA in 1763. [RGG#114]

COCHRANE, JAMES, graduated MA from Glasgow
University in 1813, Irish Presbyterian minister at Larne
1815 to 1824. [RGG#115]

COCKBURN, SIR WILLIAM JAMES, in Kinsale, 1789,
brother of James Cockburn in Glasgow.
[NAS.GD216.231]

COGHLAN, BOYLE, from Ireland, graduated MD from
Edinburgh University in 1773. [GME#11]

COHOON, JAMES, from Ireland, graduated MA from
Glasgow University in 1819. [RGG#115]

COLLES, ABRAHAM, from Ireland, graduated MD from
Edinburgh University in 1797. [GME#28]

COLLINS, JAMES, graduated MA from Glasgow University
in 1812, either an Irish Presbyterian minister at Dromore
from 1816 to 1863, who died on 19 December 1863, or an
Irish Presbyterian minister at Minterburn from 1829 to
1840, who died on 23 December 1840. [RGG#116]

COLLINS, JAMES, from Ireland, graduated MD from Edinburgh University in 1822. [GME#67]

COLLINS, ROBERT, graduated MD from Glasgow University in 1822, in Dublin then in Navan, County Meath. [RGG#116]

COLVIL, ALEXANDER, graduated MD from Glasgow University in 1728, Presbyterian minister of Dromore from 1725 to 1777, died on 23 April 1777. [RGG#117]

COLVILL, WILLIAM, from Ireland, graduated MA from Glasgow University in 1796. [RGG#117]

CONCANEN, THOMAS, from Ireland, graduated MD from Edinburgh University in 1788. [GME#20]

CONNELL, or DOUGLAS, JANET, in Tralee, testament confirmed with the Commissariat of Edinburgh on 10 April 1827. [NAS.CC8.8.151.2240]

CONNOLLY, DANIEL, from Ireland, graduated MD from Glasgow University in 1788. [RGG#119]

CONNOR, JAMES, from Ireland, graduated MA from Glasgow University in 1777. [RGG#119]

CONYNGHAM, WILLIAM LENOX, eldest son of George Lenox of Springhill, County Londonderry, graduated MA from Glasgow University in 1812. [RGG#119]

COOK, ALEXANDER, in Donaghadee, testament confirmed with the Commissariat of Edinburgh on 18 November 1813. [NAS.CC8.8.139.249]

COOK, DANIEL, from Ireland, graduated MD from Edinburgh University in 1767. [GME#9]

COOKE, DANIEL, younger son of Richard Cooke a gentleman in Dublin, matriculated at Glasgow University in 1756, graduated MA in 1758. [RGG#120]

COOKE, JAMES, graduated MD from Edinburgh University in 1821. [GME#64]

CORCORAN, THOMAS, of the Berwick Fencible Horse, married Mary Milworth, on 29 October 1799. [Ballymodan parish register, Co. Cork]

CORMICK, MICHAEL, from Ireland, graduated MA, MD, from Glasgow University in 1772. [RGG#122]

CORRY, JOHN, eldest son of Reverend John Currie of Newton Currie, Ireland, matriculated at Glasgow University in 1753, graduated MA in 1755. [RGG#122]

CORSS, ROBERT, from Ireland, graduated from Edinburgh University on 14 February 1738. [CEG#207]

COULTER, JOHN, graduated MA from Glasgow University in 1815, a Presbyterian minister at Dundonald, Belfast, died 1877. [RGG#123]

COURTNEY, JOHN, from Ireland, graduated MA from Glasgow University in 1809. [RGG#124]

COUSINS, JAMES, from Ireland, graduated MA from Glasgow University in 1787. [RGG#125]

COWAN, ANDREW, from Ireland, graduated MD from Glasgow University in 1802. [RGG#125]

COWAN, JOHN, eldest son of Joseph Cowan in Newry, County Down, matriculated at Glasgow University in 1768, graduated MA in 1772. [RGG#125]

COWAN, JOHN, graduated MA from Glasgow University in 1797, possibly an Irish Presbyterian minister at Coagh from 1801 to 1841, died 26 July 1841. [RGG#125]

COX, JOHN, son of John Cox a farmer in County Donegal, matriculated at Glasgow University in 1761, graduated MA in 1764. [RGG#126]

COX, JOHN, from Ireland, graduated MD from Edinburgh University in 1798. [GME#29]

COYLE, PATRICK, from Ireland, graduated C.M. from Glasgow University in 1819. [RGG#127]

COYNE, BARBABY, from Ireland, graduated MD from Edinburgh University in 1803. [GME#35]

CRAIG, JOHN, elder son of John Craig a merchant in the parish of Tullycorbit, County Monaghan, matriculated at Glasgow University in 1801, graduated MA in 1804. [RGG#128]

CRAIG, WILLIAM, graduated MA from Glasgow University in 1811, possibly an Irish Presbyterian minister at Carnmoney from 1819 to 1823, at Dromora from 1823 to 1871, died 22 December 1871. [RGG#129]

CRAMER, SAMUEL JOHNSTON, from Ireland, graduated MD in 1800. [RGG#129]

CRAMPTON, JOHN, from Ireland, graduated MD from Edinburgh University in 1793. [GME#24]

CRAMPTON, Sir PHILIP, born in Dublin 7 June 1777, graduated MD from Glasgow University in 1799, lecturer of Clinical Surgery in Dublin, died 10 June 1858. [RGG#129]

CRAUFORD, STEWART, from Ireland, graduated MD from Edinburgh University in 1794. [GME#26]

CRAVEN, JOHN, from Ireland, graduated MD from Edinburgh University in 1787. [GME#19]

CRAWFORD, ALEXANDER, graduated MA, MD, from Glasgow University in 1774, possibly a physician in Lisburn who died 29 August 1823 aged 68. [RGG#130]

CRAWFORD, ANDREW, fourth son of James Crawford a farmer in the parish of Killinard, County Donegal,

matriculated at Glasgow University in 1768, graduated
MA in 1769. [RGG#130]

CRAWFORD, FREDERICK, from Ireland, graduated MA in
1788. [RGG#130]

CRAWFORD, JAMES, son of James Crawford a merchant in
Donegal City, matriculated at Glasgow University in
1755, graduated MA in 1756. [RGG#131]

CRAWFORD, WILLIAM, graduated MA in 1763 and DD in
1784 from Glasgow University, Presbyterian minister at
Strabane from 1766 to 1798, and at Holywood from 1798
to 1800, died there on 4 January 1800. [RGG#132]

CREAGHE, MARTIN CONNELL, from Ireland, graduated
MD from Glasgow University in 1799. [RGG#132]

CRORY, SAMUEL, graduated MA from Glasgow University
in 1813, Irish Presbyterian minister at Drumlough, died 19
May 1861. [RGG#133]

CROZIER, JOHN, from Ireland, graduated MD from Glasgow
University in 1809. [RGG#134]

CROZIER, MATTHEW, graduated MD from Glasgow
University in 1791, later in Down, Ireland. [RGG#134]

CROZIER, WILLIAM, graduated MA from Glasgow
University in 1816, minister in Clonmel, County
Tipperary, from 1824 to 1832, in Kilmore, County Down,
from 1832 to 1872, died 22 May 1873. [RGG#134]

CRUMPE, CHRISTOPHER, from Ireland, graduated MD
from Glasgow University in 1787. [RGG#135]

CRUMPE, FRANCIS, graduated MD from Edinburgh
University in 1821. [GME#64]

CRUMPE, SAMUEL, from Ireland, graduated MD from
Edinburgh University in 1788. [GME#20]

CRYAN, PETER, from Ireland, graduated MD from Edinburgh
University in 1822. [GME#67]

CULLEN, EDMUND, from Ireland, graduated MD from
Edinburgh University in 1780. [GME#15]

CUMING, JOHN, second son of Reverend Robert Cuming the
rector of the parish of Magheraclony, County Monaghan,
matriculated at Glasgow University in 1774, graduated
MA in 1776. [RGG#136]

CUNNINGHAM, ROBERT, graduated MA from Glasgow
University in 1809, Irish Presbyterian minister at
Minterburn from 1812 to 1829, died 15 May 1829.
[RGG#138]

CUNNINGHAM, WILLIAM, graduated MA from Glasgow
University in 1820, Irish Presbyterian minister at Dundalk
from 1825 to 1829, died 15 May 1829. [RGG#138]

CUPPLES, CHARLES, graduated MD from Edinburgh
University in 1821. [GME#64]

CUPPLES, SNOWDEN, graduated MA in 1773 and DD in
1793 from Glasgow University, a minister at
Carrickfergus. [RGG#138]

CUPPLES, THOMAS, from Ireland, graduated MD from
Edinburgh University in 1777. [GME#13]

CURRY, JAMES, from Ireland, graduated MD from Edinburgh
University in 1784. [GME#17]

CURRY, JOSEPH, eldest son of John Curry a farmer in the
parish of Glendermott, County Londonderry, matriculated
at Glasgow University in 1814, graduated MA in 1817.
[RGG#140]

CURSON, ALEXANDER, from Ireland, graduated MA from
Glasgow University in 1796. [RGG#140]

CUTHBERT, EPHRAIM, son of John Cuthbert of Ballygall, a
gentleman in Dublin, matriculated at Glasgow University
in 1732, graduated MA in 1734. [RGG#140]

CUTHBERTSON, WILLIAM, graduated MA from Glasgow
University in 1809, Irish Presbyterian minister at
Cullybackey from 1818 to 1832, died 27 March 1836.
[RGG#141]

DALY, CHARLES, from Ireland, graduated MD from
Edinburgh University in 1790. [GME#22]

DALY, CORNELIUS, from Ireland, graduated MD from
Edinburgh University in 1800. [GME#31]

DALY, DANIEL, from Ireland, graduated MD from Edinburgh
University in 1774. [GME#12]

DAVIDSON, PATRICK, a licentiate of the Church of
Scotland, admitted as minister of Monreagh, County
Donegal, 9 January 1776, returned to Scotland in October
1786. [F.7.528]

DAVIES, JOHN, eldest son of Robert Davies a farmer in the
parish of Donachedy, County Tyrone, matriculated at
Glasgow University in 1776, graduated MA in 1782.
[RGG#145]

DAVIES, ROBERT, from Ireland, graduated MD from
Edinburgh University in 1757. [GME#7]

DAVIS, ANDREW, youngest son of John Davis in
Lisnavaghrey, County Down, matriculated at Glasgow
University in 1768, graduated MA in 1769. [RGG#145]

DAVIS, JAMES, graduated MA from Glasgow University in
1808, possibly an Irish Presbyterian minister at
Banbridge, ordained 1814. [RGG#146]

DAVIS, JOHN, eldest son of James Davis a wright in the parish
of Kilmore, County Down, matriculated at Glasgow
University in 1799, graduated MA in 1802. [RGG#146]

DAVIS, JOHN, graduated MA from Glasgow University in 1813, possibly an Irish Presbyterian minister at Killeter from 1828 to 1835, died 25 February 1835. [RGG#146]

DAVISON, JAMES, graduated MA from Glasgow University in 1780, possibly a Presbyterian minister at Auchnacloy and Ballygawley, County Tyrone, 1787 to 1811, died 3 february 1813. [RGG#146]

DAVISON, ROBERT, Scots-Irish, graduated MA from Glasgow University in 1731. [RGG#146]

DAVYS, JOHN, from Ireland, graduated MA from Glasgow University in 1766. [RGG#146]

DEANE, WILLIAM GODFREY, from Ireland, graduated MD from Edinburgh University in 1803. [GME#34]

DEASY, MORGAN, from Ireland, graduated MD from Glasgow University in 1785. [RGG#148]

DE BUTTS, SAMUEL, from Ireland, graduated MD from Edinburgh University in 1782. [GME#16]

DE COURCEY, JAMES, from Ireland, graduated MD from Edinburgh University in 1795. [GME#26]

DELAP, ALEXANDER, from Ireland, graduated MA from Glasgow University in 1776. [RGG#148]

DENHAM, JOSEPH, graduated MA from Glasgow University in 1767, a Presbyterian minister at Enniskillin from 1781 to 1799, and at Killeshandra from 1799 to 1834, died 21 October 1834. [RGG#148]

DENNY, DAVID, graduated MD from Edinburgh University in 1821. [GME#64]

DEVEREAUX, MICHAEL, from Ireland, graduated MD from Edinburgh University in 1822. [GME#67]

DICK, JAMES, born 7 November 1799 in Strabane, graduated MA from Glasgow University in 1818, minister at

Kellswater and professor of Systematic Theology, died 24
May 1880. [RGG#151]

DICK, WILLIAM, from Ireland, graduated MD from
Edinburgh University in 1790. [GME#22]

DICKSON, ANNA, second daughter of Reverend John
Dickson, Archdeacon of Hillsborough, County Down,
1798. [NAS.GD22.1289]

DICKSON, HUGH, fifth son of John Dickson a farmer in the
parish of Cormmeney, County Antrim, matriculated at
Glasgow University in 1778, graduated MA in 1781 and
MD in 1784. [RGG#154]

DICKSON, JOHN, eldest son of John Dickson a farmer in the
parish of Dromore, County Down, matriculated at
Glasgow University in 1810, graduated MA in 1812.
[RGG#154]

DICKSON, STEPHEN, from Ireland, graduated MD from
Edinburgh University in 1783. [GME#17]

DICKSON, WILLIAM STEEL, born 25 December 1744,
Presbyterian minister of Glastry from 1771 to 1780, Port-
a-Ferry from 1780 to 1799, Second Keady from 1803 to
1815, graduated DD from Glasgow University in 1784,
deeply implicated in the Irish Rebellion of 1798, a state
prisoner in Fort George, Scotland, for 3 years, resident of
Belfast from 1815 to 1824, died 27 December 1824.
[RGG#155]

DILL, JOHN, graduated MA from Glasgow University in 1821,
Presbyterian minister at Carnmoney, County Antrim, from
1825 to 1841, died 19 February 1841. [RGG#155]

DILL, MARCUS, graduated MD from Glasgow University in
1817 and CM in 1852, Ballykelly, County Londonderry,
sometime a surgeon in the Royal Navy, died in 1867.
[RGG#155]

DILL, RICHARD, graduated MA from Glasgow University in
1824, Presbyterian minister at Tandragee from 1829 to

1835, and at Ormond Quay, Dublin, from 1835 to 1858, died 8 December 1858. [RGG#155]

DILLON, BARTHOLEMEW, from Ireland, graduated MD from Edinburgh University in 1778. [GME#14]

DILLON, MICHAEL, from Ireland, graduated MD from Glasgow University in 1809. [RGG#156]

DILLON, THOMAS, graduated MD from Edinburgh University in 1821. [GME#64]

DIXON, JAMES, a merchant in Dublin, serviced as heir to his uncle George Swan of Garshake, a surgeon in Dunbarton, on 16 December 1825. [NAS.S/H]

DOBBIN, JAMES, from Ireland, graduated MD from Edinburgh University in 1751. [GME#4]

DONALDSON, JOHN, from Ireland, graduated MD from Edinburgh University in 1750. [GME#4]

DONNELL, JAMES, from Ireland, graduated CM from Glasgow University in 1820. [RGG#160]

DONNOGHUE, JEFFREY, second son of John Donnoghue a merchant in Cork, matriculated at Glasgow University in 1768, graduated MA in 1771. [RGG#161]

DONOVAN, JAMES, from Ireland, graduated MD from Edinburgh University in 1784. [GME#17]

DONOVAN, SAVAGE, from Ireland, graduated MD from Edinburgh University in 1796. [GME#27]

DOUGALL, DUNCAN, in Strabane, 1801. [NAS.GD13.323]

DOUGALL, GEORGE, graduated MA from Glasgow University in 1779, possibly a Presbyterian minister at Magharafelt, County Tyrone, from 1786 to 1810, died 9 December 1810. [RGG#161]

DOUGLAS, ADAM, from Ireland, graduated MD from
Edinburgh University in 1791. [GME#22]

DOUGLAS, EDMUND ALEXANDER, graduated MD from
Edinburgh University in 1821. [GME#64]

DOUGLASS, CHARLES, elder son of James Douglass in the
parish of Clough, County Antrim, matriculated at
Glasgow University in 1764, graduated MA in 1764.
[RGG#163]

DOWE, PHILIP, from Ireland, graduated MD from Edinburgh
University in 1799. [GME#31]

DOWLING, JOSEPH, from Ireland, graduated MD from
Glasgow University in 1790. [RGG#164]

DOWLING, MICHAEL, from Ireland, graduated MD from
Glasgow University in 1788. [RGG#164]

DOWNES, SYLVESTER, from Ireland, graduated MD from
Edinburgh University in 1798. [GME#29]

DRENNAN, WILLIAM, from Ireland, graduated MD from
Edinburgh University in 1778. [GME#14]

DREW, WILLIAM, from Ireland, graduated MD from
Edinburgh University in 1822. [GME#67]

DROUGHT, THOMAS, fourth son of Robert Drought a farmer
in the parish of Ballyboy, King's County, matriculated at
Glasgow University in 1770, graduated MA in 1771.
[RGG#165]

DRUMGOLE, THOMAS, from Ireland, graduated MD from
Edinburgh University in 1800. [GME#31]

DUCHAL, JAMES, born 1697, graduated DD from Glasgow
University in 1753, a Presbyterian minister in Cambridge,
in Antrim and in Dublin, died 4 May 1761. [RGG#166]

DUCK, JOHN, son of James Duck of the Caithness Legion, was baptised on 21 January 1800. [Ballymodan parish register, Co. Cork]

DUDLEY, JONATHAN, from Ireland, graduated MD from Edinburgh University in 1783. [GME#17]

DUFF, JOHN, eldest son of David Duff a merchant in the parish of Ballielogg, County Tyrone, matriculated at Glasgow University in 1787, graduated MA in 1790. [RGG#167]

DUGGAN, HUGH, from Ireland, graduated MD from Edinburgh University in 1793. [GME#24]

DUKE, VALENTINE, second son of Robert Duke a farmer in the parish of Killturrow, County Sligo, matriculated at Glasgow University in 1772, graduated MA in 1773. [RGG#168]

DUN, WILLIAM, Presbyterian minister at Killyleagh from 1745 to 1765, and at Cook Street, Dublin, graduated DD from Glasgow University in 1780. [RGG#168]

DUNBAR, JOHN, third son of John Dunbar in County Down, matriculated at Glasgow University in 1758, graduated MA in 1761. [RGG#168]

DUNCAN, EDWARD HENRY, younger son of Henry Duncan of Kilmore, County Meath, gentleman, matriculated at Glasgow University in 1763, graduated MA there in 1764. [RGG#169]

DUNCAN, JOHN, from Ireland, graduated MA from Glasgow University in 1799. [RGG#170]

DUNCAN, WILLIAM, in Ireland, 1786. [NAS.GD216.221]

DUNCAN, WILLIAM, from Ireland, graduated MD from Edinburgh University in 1822. [GME#66]

DUNCAN, ..., a merchant in Dublin and part owner of the Sally of Greenock, 1795. [NAS.CS29.907.34]

DUNDASS, JOHN, from Ireland, graduated MA from Glasgow University in 1769. [RGG#171]

DUNLAP, DANIEL, born in Ireland, a student of theology, graduated MA from Glasgow University in 1769. [RGG#171]

DUNLOP, JAMES, graduated MA from Glasgow University in 1806, an Irish Presbyterian minister at Ballyrashane from 1809 to 1830, died 16 November 1830. [RGG#171]

DUNN, JOHN, graduated NA in 1773 and LL.D. in 1785 from Glasgow University, a barrister at law and Member of the Irish House of Commons. [RGG#175]

DUNN, ROBERT, second son of Robert Dunn a farmer in the parish of St Andrews, County Down, matriculated at Glasgow University in 1811, graduated MA in 1814. [RGG#173]

EADIE, THOMAS, in Killybegs, 1745. [NAS.GD10.946]

ECCLES, SAMUEL, graduated MA from Glasgow University in 1813, an Irish Presbyterian minister at Armagh from 1817 to 1823, died 21 February 1823. [RGG#176]

ECHLIN, ARTHUR, son of Reverend John Echlin in County Antrim, matriculated at Glasgow University in 1731, graduated MA in 1732. [RGG#176]

EDGAR, SAMUEL, born 1766, graduated MA from Glasgow University in 1792, secession minister at Ballynahinch, proprietor of an academy there, graduated DD of Union College, USA in 1820, died 17 October 1826. [RGG#177]

EDWARDS, EDWARD, second son of Matthew Edwards a gentleman in the parish of Orney, County Tyrone, matriculated at Glasgow University in 1770, graduated MA in 1773. [RGG#178]

ELCOCK, NICOLAS, from Ireland, graduated MD from Edinburgh University in 1786. [GME#19]

ELDER, MATTHEW, graduated MA from Glasgow
University in 1809, an Irish Presbyterian minister at
Dunean from 1811 to 1817. [RGG#179]

ELDER, SAMUEL, graduated MA from Glasgow University in
1808, an Irish Presbyterian minister at Ballyeaston from
1813, died 21 February 1821. [RGG#179]

ELLIOT, JOHN, from Ireland, graduated MD from Edinburgh
University in 1802. [GME#34]

ELLIOT, JOHN, eldest son of Francis Elliot a farmer in the
parish of Monaghan, County Monaghan, matriculated at
Glasgow University in 1809, graduated MA in 1814.
[RGG#179]

ELLIOT, ROBERT, eldest son of John Elliot a merchant in
Monaghan town, matriculated at Glasgow University in
1780, graduated MA in 1782. [RGG#179]

ELLIOT, ROBERT, from Ireland, graduated MA from
Glasgow University in 1782. [RGG#179]

ELLISON, THOMAS, graduated MA from Glasgow
University in 1815, an Irish Presbyterian minister at
Banagher from 1822 to 1847, died 6 January 1847.
[RGG#180]

EMMET, THOMAS ADDIS, from Ireland, graduated MD
from Edinburgh University in 1784. [GME#17]

ERSKINE, SIR HARRY, in Dublin, 1762. [NAS.GD164.1694]

ERSKINE, JOHN, born 1720, fifth son of James Erskine, Lord
Grange, and Rachel Chiesley his wife, appointed Dean of
Cork. [SP.V.629]

ERSKINE, JOHN, from Ireland to Alloa, Clackmannanshire, in
1792. [NAS.GD124.15.1683]

EVANS, SAMUEL, from Ireland, graduated MA, MD, from
Glasgow University in 1773. [RGG#182]

EVANS, THOMAS, from Ireland, graduated MD from Edinburgh University in 1790. [GME#22]

EVANS, WILLIAM JONES, from Ireland, graduated MD from Edinburgh University in 1788. [GME#21]

EWING, JOHN, from Ireland, graduated MA in 1782. [RGG#183]

FAIRTLOUGH, EDWARD, from Ireland, graduated MD from Edinburgh University in 1785. [GME#18]

FALKINER, JOHN, youngest son of Frederick Falkiner a gentleman in Dublin, matriculated at Glasgow University in 1768, graduated MA in 1769. [RGG#184]

FALLON, JOHN, from Ireland, graduated MD from Edinburgh University in 1758. [GME#7]

FARRELL, CHARLES, from Ireland, graduated MD from Edinburgh University in 1798. [GME#28]

FAUCETT, RICHARD, from Ireland, graduated MD from Edinburgh University in 1796. [GME#27]

FAULKNER, ARTHUR BROOKE, from Ireland, graduated MD from Edinburgh University in 1803. [GME#35]

FAULKNER, JOHN, A.M., Dublin, graduated as a Doctor of Divinity from Edinburgh University on 24 December 1778. [CEG#245]

FAWCETT, JOHN, from Ireland, graduated MD from Edinburgh University in 1822. [GME#67]

FENNELL, CHARLES, only son of William Fennell a gentleman in Limerick, matriculated at Glasgow University in 1772, graduated MA in 1773. [RGG#185]

FERGUS, PETER WILLIAM, from Ireland, graduated MD from Edinburgh University in 1783. [GME#17]

FERGUSON, CHARLES, a merchant in Cork, husband of Ann, daughter of James Ferguson of Craigdarroch, 1793. [NAS.GD135.2084]

FERGUSON, DAVID, from Ireland, graduated CM from Glasgow University in 1823. [RGG#186]

FERGUSON, ELIZABETH, lawful daughter ot William Ferguson, schoolmaster in Carrickfergus, Ireland, and spouse to Cornet Patrick Maxwell, now town adjutant of Berwick, brother german to George Maxwell alias Napier of Kilmahew, and Patrick and James Maxwell their children, against the said Cornet Patrick Maxwell, married in Miln's Court, Bowhead of Edinburgh on 23 April 1711. [Consistorial Process and Decreet, Process of Declarator of Marriage and Adherence, 1739, Commissariat of Edinburgh]

FERGUSON, JAMES, from Ireland, graduated MA from Glasgow University in 1809. [RGG#187]

FETHERSTON, ROBERT, from Ireland, graduated MD from Glasgow University in 1786. [RGG#190]

FIDDES, JAMES, third son of Hugh Fiddes a farmer in the parish of Devenish, County Fermanagh, matriculated at Glasgow University in 1772, graduated MA in 1775. [RGG#190]

FIELD, JOHN, from Ireland, graduated MA from Glasgow University in 1764. [RGG#190]

FIFE, MARGARET, in Belfast, serviced as heiress to her cousin Janet Fife daughter of Thomas Fife in Paisley, Renfrewshire, 18 December 1779. [NAS.S/H]

FIFE, SARAH, in Belfast, serviced as heiress to her cousin Janet Fife daughter of Thomas Fife in Paisley, Renfrewshire, on 18 December 1779. [NAS.S/H]

FINLAY, JAMES, an edge tool maker in Dublin, December 1780. [NAS.CS16.1.177]

FINLAY, QUINTIN, from Ireland, graduated MA from
Glasgow University in 1767. [RGG#192]

FINLAY, SAMUEL, born in County Armagh in 1715, pastor
in Nottingham, Maryland, and head of an academy there
from 1744 to 1760, graduated DD from Glasgow
University in 1763, President of the College of Princeton,
New Jersey, from 1761 to 1766, died in Philadelphia on
17 July 1766. [RGG#193]

FINN, JOHN, from Ireland, graduated MD from Edinburgh
University in 1802. [GME#33]

FISHER, THOMAS, from Ireland, graduated MD from
Edinburgh University in 1822. [GME#67]

FITZGERALD, JOHN, from Ireland, graduated MD from
Edinburgh University in 1822. [GME#67]

FITZGERALD, THOMAS WILLIAM, from Ireland,
graduated MD from Edinburgh University in 1802.
[GME#33]

FITZPATRICK, THOMAS, from Ireland, graduated MD from
Edinburgh University in 1801. [GME#32]

FLEMING, DAVID, from Ireland, graduated MD from
Glasgow University in 1787. [RGG#195]

FLEMING, JAMES, second son of William Fleming a farmer
in the parish of Derryloran, County Tyrone, matriculated
at Glasgow University in 1807, graduated MA in 1810.
[RGG#196]

FLEMING, SAMUEL, son of Reverend James Fleming in the
parish of Shankhill, County Armagh, matriculated at
Glasgow University in 1740, graduated MA in 1743 and
MD in 1750. [RGG#196]

FLEMING, WILLIAM only son of Thomas Fleming a farmer
in the parish of Desertlin, County Londonderry,
matriculated at Glasgow University in 1803, graduated
MA in 1806. [RGG#197]

FLEMING, WILLIAM, second son of Josiah Fleming a farmer in the parish of Desertlin, County Tyrone, matriculated at Glasgow University in 1807, graduated MA in 1810. [RGG#197]

FLETCHER, JAMES, from Ireland, graduated MD from Edinburgh University in 1790. [GME#22]

FLETCHER, PHILIP, from Ireland, graduated MA from Glasgow University in 1776. [RGG#197]; from Ireland, graduated MD from Edinburgh University in 1781. [GME#16]

FLETCHER, PHILIP, from Ireland, graduated CM from Glasgow University in 1818. [RGG#197]

FLEURY, JOHN CHARLES, from Ireland, graduated MD from Edinburgh University in 1760. [GME#7]

FLOCKHART, ANDREW, a soldier of the Caithness Legion, married Catherine Brien on 21 July 1799. [Ballymodan parish register, Co. Cork]

FOGARTY, GEORGE, from Ireland, graduated MD from Edinburgh University in 1794. [GME#25]

FOLDS, WILLIAM, eldest son of John Folds minister of the parish of Killanny, County Monaghan, matriculated at Glasgow University in 1770, graduated MA in 1772. [RGG#198]

FORBES, CATHERINE, daughter of Duncan Forbes, of the Rothesay and Caithness Regiment, was baptised on 9 March 1800. [Cloyne Cathedral, Co. Cork]

FORRESTER, ROBERT, from Ireland, graduated MD from Edinburgh University in 1794. [GME#26]

FORSTER, JAMES, son of James Forster in the parish of Donaughmore, County Donegal, matriculated at Glasgow University in 1746, graduated MA in 1748. [RGG#200]

FORSTER, JAMES, from Ireland, graduated MD from
Edinburgh University in 1786. [GME#19]

FORSTER, ROBERT, from Ireland, graduated MA from
Glasgow University in 1777. [RGG#200]

FORSTER, THOMAS, second son of Arthur Forster a farmer
in the parish of Ardstraw, County Tyrone, matriculated at
Glasgow University in 1775, graduated MA in 1776.
[RGG#200]

FORSYTH, GEORGE, graduated MD in 1813, Carrickfergus,
County Antrim, died 1857. [RGG#200]

FORSYTHE, JAMES, from Ireland, graduated MD from
Edinburgh University in 1782. [GME#16]

FOSTER, EDWARD, from Ireland, graduated MD from
Edinburgh University in 1767. [GME#9]

FOWLER, GEORGE, from Ireland, graduated MD from
Edinburgh University in 1794. [GME#25]

FRAZER, WYNNE B., from Ireland, graduated MD from
Glasgow University in 1822. [RGG#205]

FRIMBLE, GEORGE, from Ireland, graduated MD from
Glasgow University in 1802. [RGG#206]

FRITH, RICHARD, from Ireland, graduated MD from
Edinburgh University in 1822. [GME#67]

FRY, CHARLES DILLON, from Ireland, graduated MD from
Edinburgh University in 1822. [GME#67]

FRYAR, THOMAS DOBBIN, eldest son of Leonard Fryar a
merchant in Cappy, County Down, matriculated at
Glasgow University in 1766, graduated MA in 1768.
[RGG#207]

FULHAM, THOMAS, from Ireland, graduated MD from
Edinburgh University in 1784. [GME#17]

FULLARTON, DAVID, graduated MA from Glasgow
University in 1754, possibly Presbyterian minister at
Carrickfergus from 1756 to 1767. [RGG#207]

GAGE, ELIZABETH, of the Kingdom of Ireland, and Daniel
McNeill, marriage settlement, 1771.
[NAS.CS16.1.134/291]

GAHAGAN, JOHN, from Ireland, graduated MD from
Edinburgh University in 1790. [GME#22]

GAHAGAN, JOSEPH, from Ireland, graduated MD from
Edinburgh University in 1791. [GME#22]

GALBRAITH, ANDREW, from Ireland, graduated MD from
Edinburgh University in 1796. [GME#27]

GALBRAITH, Captain ARTHUR, in Dublin, was admitted as
a burgess of Inveraray on 9 December 1731. [IBR]

GALBRAITH, HUMPHREY, from Ireland, graduated MA
from Glasgow University in 1782. [RGG#209]

GALBRAITH, MATHEW, third son of Hugh Galbraith in
County Tyrone, matriculated at Glasgow University in
1753, graduated MA in 1754. [RGG#209]

GALBRAITH, RICHARD, son of James Galbraith of
Cappahard, Ireland, serviced as heir to James Galbraith of
Balgair who died in May 1794, re Balgair, parts of the
barony of Bandalloch in the parish of Balfron,
Stirlingshire, 28 August 1806. [NAS.S/H]

GALWEY, ST JOHN, from Ireland, graduated MD from
Edinburgh University in 1801. [GME#32]

GAMBLE, JAMES, second son of James Gamble a farmer in
the parish of Loughgilly, County Armagh, matriculated at
Glasgow University in 1810, graduated MA in 1814.
[RGG#210]

GAMBLE, JOSIAS, graduated MD in 1787 and MA in 1797
from Glasgow University, possibly a Presbyterian

minister at Enniskillen from 1799 to 1804, then a manufacturing chemist in County Monaghan, then in Dublin, then in St Helen's, Lancashire, died 27 January 1848. [RGG#211]

GAMBLE, SAMUEL, graduated DD from Glasgow University in 1817, a Presbyterian minister at Ramelton, County Donegal. [RGG#211]

GAMBLE, WILLIAM, graduated MD from Glasgow University in 1731, a practitioner near Belfast. [RGG#211]

GARDE, HENRY, from Ireland, graduated MD from Edinburgh University in 1782. [GME#16]

GARDE, THOMAS, graduated MD from Edinburgh University in 1821. [GME#65]

GARDNER, JAMES, born in 1780, second son of James Gardner a merchant in Edinburgh, educated at the University of Glasgow, ordained to Newtonards on 4 November 1801, died in January 1812, husband of Magdalene Frazer. [F.7.529]

GARDNER, JAMES, graduated MA from Glasgow University in 1814, Irish Presbyterian minister at Clare from 1817 to 1824. [RGG#212]

GASS, ROBERT, eldest son of John Gass a merchant in Monaghan, matriculated at Glasgow University in 1805, graduated MA in 1808. [RGG#213]

GEMMELL, ROBERT, in Belfast, serviced as heir to his father Robert Gemmell a merchant there – once a weaver in Irvine, Ayrshire, 1 November 1821. [NAS.S/H]

GERNON, PETER, from Ireland, graduated MD from Glasgow University in 1785. [RGG#216]

GETTY, JAMES, a merchant in Belfast, son of the late Reverend James Getty in Inveraray, was admitted as a burgess of Inveraray on 26 August 1747. [IBR]; 17 June

1769, [NAS.CS16.1.134/307]; a merchant in Belfast, whose testament was confirmed on 26 June 1783 with the Commissariat of Edinburgh

GIBBINGS, THOMAS, from Ireland, graduated MD from Edinburgh University in 1771. [GME#10]

GIBNEY, JOHN, from Ireland, graduated MD from Edinburgh University in 1790. [GME#22]

GIBSON, ISOBEL, daughter of .... Gibson in County Down, wife of William Boyd, sailor in Saltcoats, Ayrshire, 1742. [NAS.CS16.1.69]

GIBSON, JAMES, graduated MA from Glasgow University in 1797, possibly the Irish Presbyterian minister at Lislooney from 1801 to 1834, died in December 1866. [RGG#217]

GIBSON, JANET, daughter of ....Gibson in County Down, 1742. [NAS.CS16.1.69]

GILFILLAN, JOHN, second son of Robert Gilfillan a farmer in the parish of Comber, County Londonderry, matriculated at Glasgow University in 1811, graduated MA in 1814. [RGG#220]

GILFILLAN, SAMUEL, youngest son of Joseph Gilfillan a farmer in the parish of Glendermot, County Londonderry, matriculated at Glasgow University in 1810, graduated MA in 1813. [RGG#220]

GILL, JOHN, from Ireland, graduated MD from Edinburgh University in 1748. [GME#4]

GILLKREST, JAMES, from Ireland, graduated MD from Glasgow University in 1820. [RGG#221]

GILLMER, ALEXANDER BIRCH, from Ireland, graduated CM from Glasgow University in 1822. [RGG#222]

GILLON, WILLIAM, from Ireland, graduated MA from Glasgow University in 1810. [RGG#222]

GLASGOW, BENJAMIN, from Ireland, graduated CM from Glasgow University in 1825. [RGG#223]

GLASS, JOHN, a tailor in Irvine, then a soldier in Ireland, husband of Ann Hippenstall, 1768. [NAS.GD98.1059]

GLENDY, WILLIAM, graduated MA from Glasgow University in 1806, an Irish Presbyterian minister at Ballycarry from 1812 to 1829. [RGG#224]

GODFREY, LUKE, graduated MA from Glasgow University in 1763 and DD in 1795, Rector of Middletoun, County Cork. [RGG#224]

GOING, JOHN, from Ireland, graduated MD from Edinburgh University in 1789. [GME#21]

GOOLD, SIMON, from Ireland, graduated MD from Edinburgh University in 1755. [GME#6]

GORDON, DAVID, from Ireland, graduated MA from Glasgow University in 1773. [RGG#226]

GOUDY, JAMES, second son of Reverend James Goudy in County Monaghan, matriculated at Glasgow University in 1818, graduated MA in 1821. [RGG#228]

GOULDSBURY, ALEXANDER, third son of Robert Gouldsbury a farmer in County Longford, matriculated at Glasgow University in 1771, graduated MA in 1772. [RGG#228]

GOURLEY, WALTER, eldest son of John Gourley a merchant in Cookstown, County Tyrone, matriculated at Glasgow University in 1810, graduated MA in 1813. [RGG#228]

GRAHAM, HENRY, third son of Henry Graham a farmer in the parish of Maghera, County Londonderry, matriculated at Glasgow University in 1807, graduated MA in 1809. [RGG#229]

GRAHAM, JACKSON, graduated MA in 1810, Presbyterian minister of Armoy, County Antrim, from 1814 to 1880, died 9 January 1880. [RGG#229]

GRAHAM, WILLIAM CUNNINGHAM, of Gartmore, Freeman of the Royal Corporation of Horse Breeders in County Down, 1807. [NAS.GD22.1.535]

GRANT, HENRY, son of Andrew Grant of the Caithness Legion, was baptised on 13 March 1800. [Ballymodan parish register, Co. Cork]

GRANT, STEPHEN, from Ireland, graduated MD in 1783. [RGG#233]

GRANT, WILLIAM, born 1746, youngest son of Luke Grant, a gentleman in Cork City, matriculated at Christ Church, Oxford, in 1763, matriculated at Glasgow University in 1764, graduated MA from Glasgow University in 1766. [RGG#233]

GRAVES, JAMES, from Ireland, graduated MD from Edinburgh University in 1803. [GME#35]

GRAY, JAMES, born in Ireland 25 December 1770, graduated MA from Glasgow University in 1793, a minister of Washington, New York, then of an Associate Reformed Church in Philadelphia, conductor of a Classical Academy, later settled in Baltimore to study Theology, died in Gettysburg, Pennsylvania, on 20 September 1824. [RGG#235]

GRAY, ROBERT, graduated MA from Glasgow University, possibly an Irish Presbyterian minister at Scriggan 1819-1833, and Burt 1833 -1857, died 19 October 1857. [RGG#236]

GREEN, MARLBOROUGH, Anglo-Irish, son of Robert Green of Longford, matriculated at Glasgow University in 1731, graduated MA there in 1734. [RGG#237]

GREER, WILLIAM, third son of James Greer in Saul parish, County Down, matriculated at Glasgow University in 1781, graduated there in 1782. [RGG#238]

GREIR, JAMES, from Ireland, graduated MD from Glasgow University in 1787. [RGG#239]

GREIR, JOHN, eldest son of Archibald Grier a farmer in Rashaikin parish, County Down, matriculated at Glasgow University in 1808, graduated MA there in 1811. [RGG#239]

GREIR, JOHN, eldest son of Robert Greir a farmer in Rashaikin parish, County Down, matriculated at Glasgow University in 1811, graduated MA there in 1814. [RGG#239]

GRIFFITH, JOHN, from Ireland, graduated MD from Edinburgh University in 1822. [GME#67]

GUY, MARY, from Dublin, married James Osburn, from Aberdeenshire, in Philadelphia on 3 September 1764. [Process of Declarator of Marriage and Legitimacy, Commissariat of Edinburgh, 1740]

GWYNN, GEORGE, from Urney parish in County Tyrone, matriculated at Glasgow University in 1741, graduated MA there in 1744. [RGG#242]

HADZOR, JOHN, from Ireland, graduated MD from Edinburgh University in 1753. [GME#5]

HAINING, NICHOLAS, daughter of John Haining, portioner of Glengaber, and spouse of Daniel Mellry in Ballelly, parish of Macherally, County Down, 1767. [NAS.RS.Dumfries.xx.513]

HALIDAY, ALEXANDER, born around 1728, graduated MA, MD, from Glasgow University in 1751, a physician in Belfast and a prominent politician, died 28 April 1802. [RGG#243]

HALIDAY, WILLIAM, born in Ireland, fourth son of Robert Haliday in Belfast, County Antrim, matriculated at Glasgow University in 1779, graduated MA in 1782. [RGG#243]

HALIDAY, WILLIAM, from Ireland, graduated MD from Edinburgh University in 1786. [GME#18]

HALL, PATRICK, eldest son of William Hall a farmer in County Donegal, matriculated at Glasgow University in 1763, graduated MA in 1766. [RGG#244]

HALL, WILLIAM, eldest son of Alexander Hall in the parish of Billy, County Antrim, matriculated at Glasgow University in 1772, graduated MA there in 1775. [RGG#244]

HALPIN, OLIVER, from Ireland, graduated MD from Edinburgh University in 1802. [GME#34]

HAMILL, HUGH, graduated MA from Glasgow University in 1816, an Irish Presbyterian minister at Bushmills 1820-1864, died on 31 March 1864. [RGG#245]

HAMILL, SAMUEL, youngest son of John Hamill a farmer in the parish of Billy, County Antrim, matriculated at Glasgow University in 1810, graduated MA there in 1813. [RGG#245]

HAMILTON, ANDREW, second son of Francis Hamilton gentleman in the parish of Dromore, County Tyrone, matriculated at Glasgow University in 1769, graduated MA there in 1770. [RGG#245]

HAMILTON, ROBERT, from Ireland, graduated MD from Edinburgh University in 1780. [GME#15]

HAMILTON, WILLIAM, from Ireland, graduated MD from Edinburgh University in 1779. [GME#14]

HAMILTON, WILLIAM, from Ireland, graduated MD from Edinburgh University in 1793. [GME#24]

HANAN, DENNIS, from Ireland, graduated MD from Edinburgh University in 1802. [GME#33]

HARDIMAN, MARK, from Ireland, graduated MD from Edinburgh University in 1795. [GME#26]

HARDING, ROBERT, from Ireland, graduated MD from Edinburgh University in 1782. [GME#16]

HARDING, THOMAS, from Ireland, graduated MD from Edinburgh University in 1789. [GME#21]

HARKIN, PATRICK, graduated MD from Edinburgh University in 1801. [GME#32]

HARPER, WILLIAM, son of Alexander Harper, of the Rothesay and Caithness Regiment, and his wife Isabella, was baptised on 7 October 1798. [Cloyne Cathedral, Co Cork]

HARRIS, HENRY, from Ireland, graduated MD from Edinburgh University in 1780. [GME#15]

HARRIS, RICHARD, from Ireland, graduated MD from Edinburgh University in 1762. [GME#7]

HARRISON, WILLIAM, soldier of the Caithness Legion was buried on 8 February 1797. [Ballyhea parish register, Co. Cork]

HARROLD, EDMUND JOHNES, from Ireland, graduated MD from Edinburgh University in 1797. [GME#28]

HARTE, JOSEPH, from Ireland, graduated MD from Edinburgh University in 1802. [GME#34]

HARTT, EDWARD, from Ireland, graduated MD from Edinburgh University in 1782. [GME#16]

HARVEY, WILLIAM, from Ireland, graduated MD from Edinburgh University in 1774. [GME#12]

HAXLEY, JOHN, a merchant in Dublin, was admitted as a burgess of Inveraray on 11 July 1754. [IBR]

HAYMAN, SAMUEL, from Ireland, graduated MD from Edinburgh University in 1779. [GME#14]

HENDERSON, GEORGE, a book-seller in Dublin, serviced as heir to his grandmother Rachel Spence, wife of Thomas Henderson a surgeon in Edinburgh, 5 October 1771. [NAS.S/H]

HERON, GEORGE, born 1706, licenciate of the Presbytery of Aberdeen, ordained minister at Island Magee, County Antrim, 8 August 1747, returned to Scotland in 1752, died there 2 January 1780. [F.7.530]

HILL, CHARLES, from Ireland, graduated MD from Edinburgh University in 1783. [GME#17]

HOME, JONATHAN, in Denmurray, County Antrim, 29 September 1718. [NAS.RS.Berwick#9/257-9]

HOPKINS, FRANCIS, from Ireland, graduated MD from Edinburgh University in 1777. [GME#13]

HOPKINS, GEORGE, graduated MD from Edinburgh University in 1821. [GME#65]

HORSBURGH, WILLIAM, a distiller in Athlone later in the Canongate, Edinburgh, 1762. [NAS.RS27.159.437]

HUGGINS, JOHN, from Ireland, graduated MD from Edinburgh University in 1822. [GME#68]

HUGHES, RUSSELL P., from Ireland, graduated MD from Edinburgh University in 1822. [GME#68]

HUNGERFORD, GEORGE, from Ireland, graduated MD from Edinburgh University in 1801. [GME#33]

HUNGERFORD, RICHARD JOHN HORACE, from Ireland, graduated MD from Edinburgh University in 1760. [GME#7]

HUNTER, OLIVAR, from Ireland, graduated MD from Edinburgh University in 1790. [GME#22]

HURST, ALEXANDER, born in Ireland, only son of John Hurst a merchant in Ballinamallar, Enniskillen, matriculated at Glasgow University in 1774, graduated MA in 1775. [RGG#281]

INGHAM, CHARLES, graduated MD from Edinburgh University in 1821. [GME#65]

INGHAM, DAVID, youngest son of John Ingham a minister in the parish of Kinawley, County Fermanagh, matriculated at Glasgow University in 1769, graduated MA in 1771. [RGG#284]

INNES, WILLIAM, of Red Ammon, was admitted as a burgess of Inveraray on 21 July 1741. [IBR]

IRVINE, JAMES, second son of James Irvine a farmer in the parish of Tamlaughfinlagan, County Londonderry, matriculated at Glasgow University in 1811, graduated MA in 1814. [RGG#286]

IRVINE, ROBERT, eldest son of Robert Irvine a farmer in the parish of Killevy, County Armagh, matriculated at Glasgow University in 1772, graduated MA in 1773. [RGG#286]

IRVINE, Dr THOMAS, a physician in Lisburn, Ireland, cnf 31 November 1798 Commissariat of Edinburgh

IRWIN, ARTHUR, from Ireland, graduated MD from Edinburgh University in 1799. [GME#31]

IRWINE, ROBERT ALLOT, son of William Irwine of the Berwick Fencibles, was baptised on 10 December 1798. [Ballymodan parish register, Co. Cork]

IVORY, THOMAS, from Ireland, graduated MD from Edinburgh University in 1782. [GME#16]

JACK, CHRISTIAN, widow of W. Horsburgh of Athlone, Ireland, serviced as heiress to her brother John Jack a slater in and baillie of the Canongate, 15 June 1753. [NAS.S/H]

JACK, MATTHEW, in Maggithgon, Ireland, 1776. [NAS.CS16.1.168, 256]

JACKSON, ALEXANDER, from Ireland, graduated MD from Edinburgh University in 1787. [GME#19]

JACKSON, JAMES, graduated MA from Glasgow University in 1740, an Irish Presbyterian minister at Ballybay from 1750 to 1781, died in September 1782. [RGG#288]

JACKSON, ROBERT, DONALDSON, from Ireland, graduated MD from Edinburgh University in 1791. [GME#22]

JACKSON, THOMAS, eldest son of James Jackson minister in the parish of Aghnamulin, County Monaghan, matriculated at Glasgow University in 1773, graduated MA in 1776. [RGG#288]

JAGOE, JOHN HENRY, from Ireland, graduated MD from Edinburgh University in 1822. [GME#68]

JAMES, THOMAS, a soldier of the Caithness Legion, married Margaret Splane on 22 September 1800. [Ballymodan parish register, Co. Cork]

JAMESON, BENJAMIN, third son of Andrew Jameson in the parish of Beterashane, County Londonderry, matriculated at Glasgow University in 1807, graduated MA in 1810. [RGG#290]

JARDINE, JOHN, in Clauchan, County Down, 1762. [NAS.RS.Dumfries.xix.187]

JENKINS, EVAN, youngest son of Evan Jenkins a farmer in the parish of Donaghmore, County Donegal, matriculated at Glasgow University in 1779, graduated MA in 1780. [RGG#293]

JENKINS, JOSEPH, graduated MA from Glasgow University in 1812, an Irish Presbyterian minister at Keady from 1816 to 1862, died 30 August 1862. [RGG#293]

JENNINGS, ROWAN, from Ireland, graduated MA from Glasgow University in 1776. [RGG#293]

JESSOP, GEORGE, from Ireland, graduated MD from Edinburgh University in 1789. [GME#21]

JOBSON, GEORGE, son of John and Margaret Jobson of the Rothesay Fencibles, was baptised on 6 October 1797. [St Nicholas parish register, Cork]

JOHNSON, ALLAN MOORE, from Ireland, graduated MA from Glasgow University in 1777. [RGG#294]

JOHNSON, DAVID, from Ireland, graduated Ch.B. from Glasgow University in 1819. [RGG#294]

JOHNSON, PHILIP, third son of Thomas Johnson minister of the parish of Maghregall, County Antrim, matriculated at Glasgow University in 1768, graduated MA in 1771. [RGG#294]

JOHNSON, THOMAS, from Ireland, graduated MD from Edinburgh University in 1791. [GME#23]

JOHNSON, WILLIAM, from Ireland, graduated MA from Glasgow University in 1812. [RGG#295]

JOHNSON, WILLIAM, second son of Francis Johnson a farmer in the parish of Drumboe, County Down, matriculated at Glasgow University in 1811, graduated MA in 1816. [RGG#295]

JOHNSTON, ARTHUR, of Belfast, was admitted as a burgess of Inveraray on 21 July 1741. [IBR]

JOHNSTON, CHARLES, from Ireland, graduated MD from Edinburgh University in 1785. [GME#18]

JOHNSTON, DAVID, son of David Johnston a farmer in the parish of Clogher, County Tyrone, matriculated at Glasgow University in 1780, graduated MA in 1784. [RGG#295]

JOHNSTON, FRANCIS, from Ireland, graduated MA from Glasgow University in 1795. [RGG#296]

JOHNSTON, GEORGE, Dublin, 1751. [NAS.GD164/352]

JOHNSTON, JAMES, from Ireland, graduated MD from Edinburgh University in 1790. [GME#22]

JOHNSTON, JOHN, from Ireland, graduated MD from Edinburgh University in 1776. [GME#13]

JOHNSTON, JOHN, from Ireland, graduated MD from Edinburgh University in 1794. [GME#25]

JOHNSTON, JOHN, graduated MA from Glasgow University in 1805, possibly an Irish Presbyterian minister of Cootehill from 1808 to 1811, and at Tullylish from 1811 to 1862, died 16 October 1862. [RGG#296]

JOHNSTON, PHILIP REID, from Ireland, graduated MD from Edinburgh University in 1801. [GME#33]

JOHNSTON, RICHARD, eldest son of Richard Johnston of Gillford, a gentleman in County Down, matriculated at Glasgow University in 1761, graduated MA in 1762. [RGG#297]

JOHNSTON, WILLIAM, from Ireland, graduated MA from Glasgow University in 1774. [RGG#297]

JOHNSTON, WILLIAM, second son of William Johnston a merchant in the parish of Clogher, County Tyrone, matriculated at Glasgow University in 1777, graduated MA in 1778. [RGG#298]

JOHNSTON, WILLIAM, from Ireland, graduated MD from Glasgow University in 1786. [RGG#298]

JONES, FRANCIS, from Ireland, graduated MD from Glasgow University in 1817. [RGG#299]

JUDGE, WILLIAM, son of Samuel Judge of the Caithness Legion, was baptised on 8 December 1799. [Ballymodan parish register, Co. Cork]

KEARY, PATRICK, from Ireland, graduated MD from Edinburgh University in 1774. [GME#12]

KEATING, GEORGE, from Ireland, graduated MD from Edinburgh University in 1780. [GME#15]

KEATING, WILLIAM, from Ireland, graduated MD from Edinburgh University in 1802. [GME#34]

KELL, JAMES, from Ireland, graduated CM from Glasgow University in 1820. [RGG#303]

KELLY, EDMOND, from Ireland, graduated MD from Edinburgh University in 1751. [GME#4]

KELLY, EDWARD, from Ireland, graduated MD from Edinburgh University in 1801. [GME#32]

KELLY, EDWARD, graduated MD from Edinburgh University in 1821. [GME#65]

KELLY, HUBERT, from Ireland, graduated MD from Glasgow University in 1789. [RGG#303]

KELLY, HUGH, from Ireland, graduated MD from Glasgow University in 1820. [RGG#303]

KELLY, JOHN, from Ireland, graduated MD from Glasgow University in 1791. [RGG#303]

KELLY, PATRICK, from Ireland, graduated MD from Glasgow University in 1796. [RGG#303]

KELSO, HAMILTON, only son of Henry Hamilton a merchant in Belfast, matriculated at Glasgow University in 1758, graduated MD in 1762. [RGG#304]

KENNEDY, HENRY, from Ireland, graduated MD from Edinburgh University in 1799. [GME#30]

KENNEDY, JOHN, eldest son of Hugh Kennedy of Cultra, a gentleman in County Down, matriculated at Glasgow University in 1763, graduated MA in 1766. [RGG#305]

KENNEDY, JOHN, only son of James Kennedy, a farmer in the parish of Aghadery, County Down, matriculated at Glasgow University in 1807, graduated MA in 1810 and MD in 1814 from Glasgow University. [RGG#305]

KENNEDY, THOMAS, graduated MA from Glasgow University in 1767, possibly a minister in America, then an Irish Presbyterian minister of Holywood from 1778 to 1788, died 7 February 1788. [RGG#306]

KENNEY, JOHN, vicar general of Cork, 1793. [NAS.GD154.683/10]

KENNY, JAMES, son of James Kenny of the Elgin Fencibles, was buried on 29 November 1798. [Ballyhea parish register, Co. Cork]

KEON, JOHN, from Ireland, graduated MD from Glasgow University in 1795. [RGG#307]

KER, ANDREW, from Ireland, graduated MD from Edinburgh University in 1790. [GME#22]

KER, JAMES, a Scots-Irishman, graduated from the University of Edinburgh on 25 February 1735. [CEG#206]

KER, MOSES, son of Samuel Ker in the parish of Tullylish, County Down, matriculated at Glasgow University in 1735, graduated MA in 1748. [RGG#307]

KERR, JAMES, graduated MA in 1776 or in 1778, possibly the Irish Presbyterian minister at Clougherney from 1781 to 1823, died 5 June 1823. [RGG#308]

KERR, ROBERT, from Ireland, graduated MA from Glasgow
University in 1794. [RGG#309]

KHEOGH, DIONYS, from Ireland, graduated MD from
Edinburgh University in 1783. [GME#17]

KIERNAN, FRANCIS, eldest son of Fergus Kiernan a farmer
in the parish of Killishandra, County Cavan, matriculated
at Glasgow University in 1769, graduated MA in 1771.
[RGG#310]

KIERNAN, RICHARD, from Ireland, graduated MD from
Edinburgh University in 1783. [GME#16]

KILLEN, JOHN, son of James Killen in County Tyrone,
matriculated at Glasgow University in 1734, graduated
MA in 1735, [RGG#310]

KINCHELA, LUDOVICK C., from Ireland, graduated MD
from Edinburgh University in 1822. [GME#68]

KING, HENRY, son of Charles King a gentleman in Dublin,
matriculated at Glasgow University in 1766, graduated
MA in 1767. [RGG#312]

KING, JOHN, licentiate of the Presbytery of St Andrews,
ordained minister at Dromara 14 December 1726, died 9
November 1762. [F.7.531]

KING, JOHN, graduated MA from Glasgow University in
1820, a Presbyterian minister at Ballyjamesduff and later
at Bellasis, Virginia, County Cavan. [RGG#312]

KINNEIR, JAMES, from Ireland, graduated MD from
Glasgow University in 1814. [RGG#313]

KIRBY, JAMES, from Ireland, graduated MD from Edinburgh
University in 1796. [GME#27]

KIRKBY, RICHARD, from Ireland, graduated MD from
Edinburgh University in 1800. [GME#32]

KIRKLAND, HUGH, fourth son of Hugh Kirkland in Market Hill, County Armagh, matriculated at Glasgow University in 1812, graduated MA in 1815. [RGG#314]

KIRKPATRICK, JAMES, graduated MD, DD, from Glasgow University in 1732, a Presbyterian minister at Templepatrick and later in Belfast, died in 1743. [RGG#314]

KIRKWOOD, ROBERT, graduated MA from Glasgow University in 1818, minister of Holywood, died 10 October 1844. [RGG#315]

KIRWAN, JAMES, graduated MD from Edinburgh University in 1821. [GME#65]

KITTSON, GEORGE RICHARD, from Ireland, graduated MD from Edinburgh University in 1788. [GME#21]

KNIGHT, THOMAS, Mayor of Youghal, 1730. [NAS.AC9.1116]

KNOX, ANDREW, son of Reverend Francis Knox in Castle Blany, County Monaghan, matriculated at Glasgow University in 1737, graduated MA in 1740. [RGG#316]

KNOX, HENRY, son of John Knox a merchant in Sligo town, matriculated at Glasgow University in 1746, graduated MA in 1749. [RGG#316]

KNOX, JAMES, graduated MA from Glasgow University in 1784, Irish Presbyterian minister at Drumbanagher from 1789 to 1794, and at Donaghadee from 1794 to 1798, died 22 March 1801. [RGG#316]

KYD, HENRY, graduated MA from Glasgow University in 1809, an Irish Presbyterian minister at Boveva from 1818 to 1839, died 4 June 1839. [RGG#317]

KYD, JOHN, brother of Henry Kyd (above), graduated MA from Glasgow University in 1809. [RGG#317]

LABATT, SAMUEL BELL, from Ireland, graduated MD from Edinburgh University in 1797. [GME#28]

LAIRD, SAMUEL, son of James Laird in the parish of Desmartin, County Londonderry, matriculated at Glasgow University in 1749, graduated MA in 1751. [RGG#319]

LANAUZE, ALEXANDER, second son of George Lanauze a merchant in Dublin, matriculated at Glasgow University in 1767, graduated MA in 1768. [RGG#320]

LANDER, JOHN, from Ireland, graduated MD from Edinburgh University in 1758. [GME#7]

LANDER, WILLIAM, from Ireland, graduated MD from Edinburgh University in 1800. [GME#32]

LANE, ABSOLOM, in Dublin, 1801. [NAS.GD13.313]

LANG, SAMUEL, from Ireland, graduated MA from Glasgow University in 1795. [RGG#322]

LANGFORD, JOHN, from Ireland, graduated MD from Edinburgh University in 1791. [GME#22]

LANPHIER, SIMON, from Ireland, graduated MD from Edinburgh University in 1778. [GME#14]

LAPSLEY, WILLIAM, youngest son of William Lapsley a farmer in County Tyrone, matriculated at Glasgow University in 1771, graduated MA in 1772. [RGG#323]

LARKIN, WILLIAM, in Tullamore, 1801. [NAS.GD13.321]

LATHAM, JOHN, from Ireland, graduated MD from Edinburgh University in 1802. [GME#33]

LAUDER, or CRAWFORD, MARGARET, in Dublin, serviced as heiress to her sister Euphemia Crawford, widow of Robert Gray a merchant in Edinburgh, 30 July 1783. [NAS.S/H]

LAW, JOHN, from Ireland, graduated MD from Edinburgh University in 1762. [GME#4]

LAW, MICHAEL, from Ireland, graduated MD from Edinburgh University in 1748. [GME#3]

LAW, MICHAEL, only son of Joseph Law a farmer in the parish of Kilcare, County Donegal, matriculated at Glasgow University in 1772, graduated MA in 1773. [RGG#324]

LAWDER, RHYND, graduated MD from Edinburgh University in 1821. [GME#65]

LAWLOR, ALEXANDER, from Ireland, graduated MD from Edinburgh University in 1801. [GME#33]

LAWRENCE, THOMAS, a banker in Coleraine, 3 May 1826. [NAS.B2/2.4.23]

LECKY, WILLIAM, from Ireland, graduated MD from Edinburgh University in 1787. [GME#19]

LEDGER, WILLIAM, from Ireland, graduated MD from Edinburgh University in 1792. [GME#23]

LEE, CADWALLADER BLANEY, from Ireland, graduated MD from Edinburgh University in 1779. [GME#14]

LEEPER, THOMAS, second son of Robert Leeper a farmer in the parish of Stanorlane, County Donegal, matriculated at Glasgow University in 1776, graduated MA in 1777. [RGG#327]

LEITCH, GEORGE, eldest son of William Leitch a farmer in the parish of Ardstraw, County Tyrone, matriculated at Glasgow University in 1766, graduated MA in 1769. [RGG#328]

LEITCH, THOMAS, graduated MA from Glasgow University in 1769, possibly a Presbyterian minister at Douglas and Clady, County Tyrone. [RGG#329]

LELAND, JOHN, born in Wigan, Lancashire, graduated MA from Glasgow University in 1734, graduated DD from Aberdeen University, a Presbyterian minister in Dublin from 1716 to 1766, died 16 January 1766. [RGG#329]

LENNOX, SARAH, born in Dublin on 22 August 1792, daughter of Charles Lennox, Duke of Lennox, and Charlotte Gordon his wife, married Sir Peregrine Maitland, died 8 September 1873. [SP.V.367]

LESLIE, ALEXANDER, in Belfast, 1795. [NAS.GD13.219]

LESLIE, DAVID, and his wife Rebecca, in Donaghadee, County Down, 1796. [NAS.GD26.13.789]

LESLIE, JAMES, in Ireland, testament confirmed with the Commissariat of Edinburgh on 18 November 1818. [NAS.CC8.8.136/170]

LEWIS, THOMAS, graduated MD from Edinburgh University in 1821. [GME#65]

LHOYD, PLUNKETT, from Ireland, graduated MD from Edinburgh University in 1770. [GME#10]

LIGHTBODY or ROBINSON, RUTH, in Belfast, daughter of Robert Lightbody, a hatter in Ayr, and his wife Janet Wilson, 1788. [NAS.S/H]

LINDSAY, BENJAMIN, from Ireland, graduated MA from Glasgow University in 1781, [RGG#332]

LINDSAY, CHARLES DALRYMPLE, born 15 December 1760, son of James the Earl of Balcarres, graduated BA in 1783 and MA in 1786 from Oxford University, and DD from Glasgow University in 1804, vicar of Sutterton, Lancashire, 1793, Dean of Killaloe and Killanore in 1803, Bishop of Kildare from 1804 to 1846, married (1) Elizabeth Fydell, (2) Catherine Coussmaker, died 8 August 1846. [RGG#332][SP.I.526]

LINDSEY, WILLIAM, eldest son of John Lindsay a farmer in the parish of Killileagh, County Down, matriculated at

Glasgow University in 1765, graduated MA in 1768.
[RGG#333]

LINN, ALLAN, from Ireland, graduated CM from Glasgow
University in 1820. [RGG#333]

LISTER, JOHN, son of George Lister in the parish of Newry,
County Down, matriculated at Glasgow University in
1751, graduated MA in 1754. [RGG#334]

LISTER, WILLIAM, second son of John Lister a farmer in the
parish of Kilmore, County Monaghan, matriculated at
Glasgow University in 1802, graduated MA in 1806.
[RGG#334]

LITTLE, JOSEPH, graduated MA from Glasgow University in
1765, a Presbyterian minister at Killyleagh from 1768 to
1813, also a medical practitioner, died in July 1813.
[RGG#334]; graduated MD from Edinburgh University in
1780. [GME#15]

LIVINGSTONE, SAMUEL, eldest son of John Livingstone a
farmer in the parish of Drumagh, County Down,
matriculated at Glasgow University in 1800, graduated
MA in 1806. [RGG#335]

LLOYD, THOMAS, second son of Owen Lloyd a gentleman in
the parish of Augrim, County Roscommon, matriculated
at Glasgow University in 1778, graduated MA in 1779.
[RGG#337]

LOANE, GEORGE, from Ireland, graduated MD from
Edinburgh University in 1822. [GME#68]

LOCKHART, GEORGE, third son of George Lockhart a
farmer in the parish of Killivy, County Armagh,
matriculated at Glasgow University in 1805, graduated
MA in 1808. [RGG#337]

LONGFIELD, JOHN, from Ireland, graduated MD from
Edinburgh University in 1759. [GME#7]

LOVE, ANNE, daughter of John Love a soldier of the Caithness legion, was baptised on 10 November 1799. [Ballymodan parish register, Co. Cork]

LOVE, WILLIAM, third son of Charles Love a farmer in the parish of Ardstraw, County Tyrone, matriculated at Glasgow University in 1812, graduated MA in 1815. [RGG#342]

LOWRY, GAVIN, only son of Thomas Lowry a farmer in the parish of Taughtoyn, County Donegal, matriculated at Glasgow University in 1771, graduated MA in 1774. [RGG#343]

LOWRY, JAMES, fourth son of James Lowry a farmer in the parish of Dungien, County Londonderry, matriculated at Glasgow University in 1762, graduated MA in 1765. [RGG#343]

LUBY, JOHN, from Ireland, graduated MD from Edinburgh University in 1803. [GME#34]

LUCAS, DANIEL, fourth son of the late Francis Lucas a gentleman in the parish of Dromore, County Monaghan, matriculated at Glasgow University in 1775, graduated MA in 1777. [RGG#343]

LUCAS, EDWARD, son of the Reverend William Lucas in Newry, County Down, matriculated at Glasgow University in 1766, graduated MA in 1768. [RGG#343]

LYLE, ROBERT, second son of Robert Lyle a farmer in the parish of Killeronaghan, County Londonderry, matriculated at Glasgow University in 1810, graduated MA in 1812. [RGG#344]

LYLE, WILLIAM, graduated MA from Glasgow University in 1811, an Irish Presbyterian minister at Dunboe from 1814 to 1867, died 3 April 1867. [RGG#344]

LYNCH, FREDERICK THADDEUS, from Ireland, graduated MD from Edinburgh University in 1799. [GME#30]

LYNCH, JOSEPH, from Ireland, graduated MD from Edinburgh University in 1802. [GME#33]

LYNCH, MARTIN, from Ireland, graduated MD from Edinburgh University in 1790. [GME#22]

LYNCH, PATRICK, from Ireland, graduated MD from Edinburgh University in 1822. [GME#68]

LYNCH, WILLIAM, from Ireland, graduated MD from Edinburgh University in 1802. [GME#33]

LYNDON, CHARLES COBBE, from Ireland, graduated BA from Glasgow University in 1777. [RGG#345]

LYNN, JAMES, second son of William Lynn a farmer in the parish of Coleraine, County Londonderry, matriculated at Glasgow University in 1810, graduated MA in 1813. [RGG#345]

LYONS, FRANCIS, graduated MD from Edinburgh University in 1821. [GME#65]

MCADAM, DAVID HASTINGS, from Ireland, graduated MD from Edinburgh University in 1822. [GME#68]

MCADAM, JAMES, graduated MD from Glasgow University in 1790, possibly an Irish Presbyterian minister at Lislooney 1787-1788. [RGG#346]

MCALISTER, JOHN, a merchant in Dublin, 1775. [NAS.CS16.1.165/411; 168/13]

MCARTHUR, DUNCAN, son of John McArthur a minister in County Antrim, matriculated at Glasgow University in 1730, graduated MA in 1732. [RGG#347]

MCAULAY, JAMES, from Ireland, graduated MA from Glasgow University in 1788. [RGG#349]

MCAULAY, JOHN, from Ireland, graduated MA in 1788. [RGG#349]

MCAULAY, JOHN, graduated MA from Glasgow University in 1816, an Irish Presbyterian minister at Donaghadee from 1822 to 1879, died 27 February 1879. [RGG#349]

MCAY, JOHN, from Ireland, graduated MA from Glasgow University in 1775. [RGG#349]

MCBRIDE, DAVID, born in Ballymoney 26 April 1726, graduated MD from Glasgow University in 1764, a surgeon of the Royal Navy, then a physician in Ballymoney and later in Dublin, died in Dublin 28 December 1778. [RGG#350]

MCCALLEN, WILLIAM, from Ireland, graduated Ch.B from Glasgow University in 1820. [RGG#350]

MCCAMBRIDGE, GEORGE, from Ireland, graduated MD from Edinburgh University in 1797. [GME#28]

MCCAMMON, JAMES, from Ireland, graduated MD from Edinburgh University in 1800. [GME#32]

MCCANCE, JOHN, graduated MA from Glasgow University in 1783, a Presbyterian minister at Comber, County Down, from 1790 to 1843, died 4 November 1843. [RGG#351]

MCCANCE, WILLIAM, graduated MA from Glasgow University in 1815, son of John McCance (above), a Presbyterian minister at Waterford until 1864, died 22 June 1882. [RGG#352]

MCCARTER, JAMES, from Ireland, graduated MA from Glasgow University in 1777. [RGG#352]

MCCARTHY, DENNIS, from Ireland, graduated MD from Edinburgh University in 1798. [GME#30]

MCCARTNEY, ALICE, daughter of James McCartney, son of James McCartney, judge of the Court of Common Pleas in Ireland, 1772. [NAS.RS.Dumfries.xxi.48]

MCCARTNEY, CATHERINE, daughter of James McCartney, son of James McCartney, judge of the Court of Common Pleas in Ireland, 1772. [NAS.RS.Dumfries.xxi.48]

MCCARTNEY, FRANCES, daughter of James McCartney, son of James McCartney, judge of the Court of Common Pleas in Ireland, and spouse of Fulk Grevile of Wellburrow, Wiltshire, 1772. [NAS.RS.Dumfries.xxi.48]

MCCARTNEY, FRANCIS, from Ireland, graduated MD from Edinburgh University in 1796. [GME#27]

MCCARTNEY, JAMES, judge of the Court of Common Pleas in Ireland, 1772. [NAS.RS.Dumfries.xxi.48]

MCCARTNEY, JAMES, son of James McCartney, judge of the Court of Common Pleas in Ireland, 1772. [NAS.RS.Dumfries.xxi.48]

MCCAW, ARTHUR, graduated Ch.B. from Glasgow University in 1820, Bushmills, County Antrim. [RGG#352]

MCAY, SAMUEL, from Ireland, graduated MD from Edinburgh University in 1785. [GME#18]

MCCAY, WILLIAM, fourth son of William McCay a farmer in the parish of Bovevesh, County Londonderry, matriculated at Glasgow University in 1807, graduated MA in 1819. [RGG#353]

MCCLARAN, ELINOR, daughter of Hugh McClarran of the Elgin Fencibles, was buried on 14 October 1798. [Ballyhea parish register, Co. Cork]

MCCLELLAND, GEORGE, graduated MA from Glasgow University in 1805, an Irish Presbyterian minister at Agoghill from 1810 to 1850, died 15 February 1850. [RGG#353]

MCCLELLAND, JAMES, graduated MA from Glasgow University in 1809, an Irish Presbyterian minister at Ballynahinch from 1812 to 1829. [RGG#353]

MCCLENACHAN, GEORGE, from Ireland, graduated MD
from Edinburgh University in 1781. [GME#16]

MCCLENAGHAN, WILLIAM, born in 1791, youngest son of
William McClenaghan a farmer in Desirtoghill, County
Londonderry, graduated MA from Glasgow University in
1810, licentiate of the Presbytery of Glasgow, ordained as
a minister at Moville 19 December 1820, died in January
1824. [F.7.531][RGG#353]

MCCLEVERTY, WILLIAM, third son of William
McCleverty in Carrickfergus, matriculated at Glasgow
University in 1764, graduated MA in 1767. [RGG#353]

MCCLOUD, CHRISTIAN, daughter of William McCloud of
the Elgin Fencibles, was buried on 12 December 1798.
[Ballyhea parish register, Co. Cork]

MCCOMB, HUGH, graduated CM from Glasgow University in
1818, Larne, County Antrim. [RGG#355]

MCCORMICK, JOHN, from Ireland, graduated MA from
Glasgow University in 1814. [RGG#356]

MCCORMICK, WILLIAM, from Ireland, graduated MA from
Glasgow University in 1765. [RGG#356]

MCCORMICK, WILLIAM JAMES, graduated MD from
Edinburgh University in 1821. [GME#65]

MCCOY, MARY, daughter of Thomas McCoy of the Caithness
Legion, was baptised on 4 March 1800. [Ballymodan
parish Register, Co. Cork]

MCCREA, WILLIAM, eldest son of William McCrea a
merchant in Down Patrick, County Down, matriculated at
Glasgow University in 1771, graduated MA in 1774.
[RGG#357]

MCCULLOCH, JAMES, son of John McCulloch a merchant
in Larne, was admitted as a burgess of Inveraray on 11
April 1727. [IBR]

MCCULLOCH, JAMES, a merchant in Belfast, owner of the Mary, galley, 1726. [NAS.AC7.32.116-213]

MCCULLOCH, WILLIAM, a watchmaker in Belfast, 1752. [NAS.CS16.1.88/338]

MCCULLAGH, JOHN, third son of Thomas McCullagh a merchant in County Monaghan, matriculated at Glasgow University in 1817, graduated MA in 1821. [RGG#358]

MCCULLAGH, WILLIAM D., eldest son of John McCullagh a farmer in the parish of Cumber, County Down, matriculated at Glasgow University in 1807, graduated MA in 1810. [RGG#359]

MCCULLY, JOHN, from Ireland, graduated MD from Edinburgh University in 1790. [GME#22]

MCCURDY, CHARLES, graduated MA from Glasgow University in 1768, an Irish Presbyterian minister at Glennan from 1783 to 1823, died 19 February 1823. [RGG#359]

MCCURLEY, ROBERT, from Ireland, graduated CM from Glasgow University in 1825. [RGG#359]

MCDERMOT, HUGH, from Ireland, graduated MD from Glasgow University in 1784. [RGG#359]

MCDERMOTT, BERNARD, from Ireland, graduated MD from Edinburgh University in 1803. [GME#35]

MCDERMOTT, PATRICK, from Ireland, graduated MD from Glasgow University in 1804. [RGG#359]

MCDONALD, BIKER, from Ireland, graduated MD from Edinburgh University in 1786. [GME#18]

MCDONALD, EDWARD LAWSON, from Ireland, graduated CM in 1825. [RGG#361]

MCDONNELL, FERGUS MCVEAGH, from Ireland, graduated MD from Glasgow University in 1788. [RGG#363]

MCDONNELL, JAMES, from Ireland, graduated MD from Edinburgh University in 1784. [GME#17]

MCDONNELL, JOHN, from Ireland, graduated MD from Edinburgh University in 1755. [GME#4]

MCDONNELL, JOHN, a merchant in Dublin, 1798. [NAS.AC7/72]

MCDONNELL, WILLIAM, son of John McDonnell of the Elgin Fencibles and Phebe Burk, residing in Maypole Road, Cork, was baptised on 12 July 1797. [St Nicholas parish register, Cork]

MCDOWALL, BENJAMIN, from Dublin, graduated as a Doctor of Divinity from Edinburgh University on 22 January 1789. [CEG#247]

MCDOWALL, JOHN, Captain of the Enniskillen Dragoons, serviced as heir to his uncle Andrew Wallace of Woolmet, Writer to the Signet, 29 April 1767. [NAS.S/H]; testament confirmed with the Commissariat of Edinburgh on 10 October 1804. [NAS.CC8.8.135.285]

MCDOWEL, JOHN, Scots-Irish, graduated MA from Glasgow University in 1731. [RGG#365]

MCDOWELL WILLIAM HENRY, second son of Hugh McDowell a schoolmaster in Donaghadee, matriculated at Glasgow University in 1819, graduated MA in 1821. [RGG#365]

MCELHENNY, JOHN, third son of John McElhenny a farmer in the parish of Donougheady, County Tyrone, matriculated at Glasgow University in 1808, graduated MA in 1811. [RGG#365]

MCEWEN, ALEXANDER, graduated MA from Glasgow University in 1813, an Irish Presbyterian minister at

Kirkcubbin from 1817 to 1837, died 29 January 1839.
[RGG#366]

MCEWEN, GEORGE, graduated MA from Glasgow
University in 1779, a Presbyterian minister at Killinchy,
County Down, from 1783 to 1795, died 20 March 1795.
[RGG#366]

MCEWAN, ROBERT, master of the Margaret of Larne, 1750.
[NAS.CS16.1.84/41]

MCGACHEY, BENJAMIN, from Ireland, graduated MD from
Glasgow University in 1790. [RGG#370]

MCGEARY, THOMAS, from Ireland, graduated MA from
Glasgow University in 1790. [RGG#371]

MCGEE, HENRY, third son of Hugh McGee in County
Londonderry, matriculated at Glasgow University in 1756,
graduated MA in 1757. [RGG#371]

MCGEE, ROBERT, from Ireland, graduated CM from
Glasgow University in 1821. [RGG#371]

MCGEOGH, JOSHUA, eldest son of William McGeogh a
merchant in Armagh city, matriculated at Glasgow
University in 1765, graduated MA in 1767. [RGG#371]

MCGHEE, ROBERT, from Ireland, graduated MA from
Glasgow University in 1764. [RGG#371]

MCGILL, JAMES, from Ireland, graduated CM from Glasgow
University in 1825. [RGG#372]

MCGOWAN, FRANCIS, eldest son of Samuel McGowan a
farmer in the parish of Derryloran, County Tyrone,
matriculated at Glasgow University in 1810, graduated
MA in 1814. [RGG#373]

MCGOWAN, JOHN, graduated MA from Glasgow University
in 1814, possibly the John G. Magowan an Irish
Presbyterian minister at Orritor from 1825 to 1867, who
died 19 September 1867. [RGG#373]

MCGOWN, HARRY, late of Donaghadee, died in Balgowan in March 1795. [Kirkmaiden gravestone, Wigtownshire]

MCGUIRE, PETER, from Ireland, graduated MD from Edinburgh University in 1802. [GME#34]

MCHUGH, TULLY, from Ireland, graduated MD from Edinburgh University in 1796. [GME#27]

MCILWAINE, JAMES, from Ireland, graduated MD from Edinburgh University in 1787. [GME#19]

MCKAY, THOMAS, born 1755, graduated MA from Glasgow University in 1781, possibly the Presbyterian minister at Brigh, County Tyrone, from 1788 to 1821, died 19 December 1821. [RGG#382]

MCKEE, ALEXANDER, graduated MA from Glasgow University in 1729, an Irish Presbyterian minister at Drum from 1733 to 1761, and at Ballieborough, died there on 13 May 1761. [RGG#383]

MCKEE, ALEXANDER, third son of Reverend Alexander McKee in County Monaghan, matriculated at Glasgow University in 1761, graduated MA in 1763. [RGG#383]

MCKEE, JOHN, from Ireland, graduated CM from Glasgow University in 1820. [RGG#383]

MCKEE, JOSEPH, graduated MA from Glasgow University in 1818, a Presbyterian minister at Killead, from 1826 to 1849, died in 1856. [RGG#383]

MCKEE, WILLIAM, from Ireland, graduated CM from Glasgow University in 1822. [RGG#383]

MCKEEN, WILLIAM, eldest son of Thomas McKeen a farmer in the parish of Ahoghill, County Antrim, matriculated at Glasgow University in 1784, graduated MA in 1789. [RGG#383]

MCKENZIE, DANIEL, son of John and Mary McKenzie of the Caithness Legion, was baptised on 14 April 1799. [St Nicholas parish register, Cork]

MCKENZIE, GEORGE, a soldier of the Rothesay and Caithness Fencibles, married Margaret Manning on 15 June 1799. [Cloyne Cathedral, Co Cork]

MCKENZIE, MARY, daughter of Hugh McKenzie a soldier of the Caithness Legion, was baptised on 22 September 1799. [Ballymodan parish register, Co. Cork]

MCKENZIE, MARY, wife of W. Benson in Belfast, serviced as heiress to her father Alexander Mackenzie, a tailor in South Carolina, 13 January 1819. [NAS.S/H]

MCKEOGH, PIERCE, from Ireland, graduated MD from Edinburgh University in 1800. [GME#32]

MCKEOWN, WILLIAM, second son of John McKeown a farmer in the parish of Killinchy, County Down, matriculated at Glasgow University in 1810, graduated MD in 1813. [RGG#387]

MCKIBBIN, THOMAS, from Ireland, graduated CM from Glasgow University in 1823. [RGG#387]

MCKIE, JOHN, of Tullygrully, Ireland, was serviced as heir to his cousin John Alexander of Drummochreen, 28 April 1809. [NAS.S/H]

MCKINLIE, ALEXANDER, from Ireland, graduated MD from Edinburgh University in 1749. [GME#4]

MCLAINE, ARCHIBALD, born in Monaghan in 1722, graduated MA and DD from Glasgow University in 1746 and 1767 respectively, minister of the Scots Kirk at the Hague, the Netherlands, from 1747 to 1796, died in Bath, England, on 25 November 1804. [RGG#393]

MCLAREN, DUNCAN, at Loughrea, 1801. [NAS.GD13.314]

MCLAUGHLIN, JOHN, graduated MA from Glasgow
University in 1817, an Irish Presbyterian minister at
Drumachose from 1824 to 1831, died 3 November 1831.
[RGG#394]

MCLEANE, JOHN, in Antrim, 1708. [NAS.GD154.677/4]

MCLEANE, LACHLAN, from Ireland, graduated MD from
Edinburgh University in 1755. [GME#6]

MCLEANE, LAUCHLINE, born in Ireland during 1727,
graduated MD from Edinburgh University in 1755, settled
in Pennsylvania, died 1778. [SA#183]

MCLOUGHLIN, PETER, from Ireland, graduated MD from
Edinburgh University in 1796. [GME#27]

MCMEACHAN, JOHN, probationer governor of Arthur
Johnston of Belfast, was admitted as a burgess of
Inveraray on 21 July 1741. [IBR]

MCMECHAN, ARTHUR, second son of Alexander
McMechan a farmer in County Down, matriculated at
Glasgow University in 1773, graduated MA in 1777.
[RGG#402]

MCMICHAN, JOHN, from Ireland, graduated MD from
Edinburgh University in 1748. [GME#3]

MCMILLAN, JAMES, eldest son of John McMillan a farmer
in the parish of Athaloe, County Tyrone, matriculated at
Glasgow University in 1813, graduated CM in 1826.
[RGG#402]

MCMORRAN, JOHN, third son of John McMorran of
Drumcaw in the parish of Donagh, County Monaghan,
matriculated at Glasgow University in 1781, graduated
MD in 1784. [RGG#403]

MCMULLAN, THOMAS, from Ireland, matriculated at
Glasgow University in 1728, graduated MA in 1730.
[RGG#403]

MCMULLAN, THOMAS, from Ireland, graduated MD from Edinburgh University in 1797. [GME#27]

MCNAMARA, BERNARD SHEEDY, from Ireland, graduated MD from Glasgow University in 1799. [RGG#405]

MCNEILL, ARCHIBALD, a surgeon apothecary in Belfast, serviced as heir to his uncle there Neil McNeill a surgeon apothecary, 18 August 1747. [NAS.S/H]; 1751. [NAS.CS16.1.85/299]

MCNEILL, GRIZEL, serviced as heiress to her father Archibald McNeill a surgeon in Belfast on 16 June 1753. [NAS.S/H]

MCNEILL, ROGER HAMILTON, in Newgrove, County Down, then in Dublin, testament confirmed on 21 January 1789 Commissariat of Edinburgh

MCNEILLY, WILLIAM, graduated MA from Glasgow University in 1745, probably the William McNeill, an Irish Presbyterian minister at Clogher from 1754 to 1770. [RGG#407]

MCONCHY, GEORGE, second son of John Maconchy in County Londonderry, matriculated at Glasgow University in 1770, graduated MA in 1774. [RGG#409]

MCPHARLAN, JOHN, from Ireland, graduated CM from Glasgow University in 1824. [RGG#409]

MCPHERSON, KENNETH, in Belfast, 1772. [NAS.GD427.203]

MCPHERSON, THOMAS, in Dublin, 1801. [NAS.GD13.307]

MCROBERTS, JOHN, from Ireland, graduated MD from Glasgow University in 1803. [RGG#412]

MCTERNAN, PATRICK, from Ireland, graduated MD from Edinburgh University in 1822. [GME#68]

MCWILLIAMS, JAMES, graduated MA at Glasgow University in 1816, an Irish Presbyterian minister at Maguiresbridge from 1822 to 1860, died 20 April 1860. [RGG#414]

MADILL, ROBERT, son of Alexander Madill a merchant in Down, Ireland, matriculated at Glasgow University in 1737, graduated MA in 1740. [RGG#415]

MAGILL, JAMES, fourth son of William Magill a merchant in Cookstown, in the parish of Derryloran, County Tyrone, matriculated at Glasgow University in 1807, graduated MA in 1810. [RGG#415]

MAGILL, ROBERT, born 7 September 1788, graduated MA at Glasgow University in 1816, a Presbyterian minister at Antrim from 1820 to 1839, died 19 February 1839. [RGG#415]

MAGRANE, PATRICK, from Ireland, graduated MD from Edinburgh University in 1797. [GME#28]

MAHAFFY, ROBERT, second son of Ninian Mahaffy a farmer in the parish of Donaughmore, County Donegal, matriculated at Glasgow University in 1769, graduated MA in 1771. [RGG#415]

MAINE, WILLIAM, eldest son of Samuel Maine a farmer in County Down, matriculated at Glasgow University in 1763, graduated MA in 1770. [RGG#416]

MAIRS, JAMES, fourth son of John Mairs in Drumleck, parish of Muckno, County Monaghan, matriculated at Glasgow University in 1787, graduated MA in 1788. [RGG#417]

MALCOM, ANDREW GEORGE, born 15 September 1782, graduated MA in 1802 and DD in 1819 from Glasgow University, Presbyterian minister at Dunmurry from 1807 to 1808, at Newry from 1809 to 1823, died 12 January 1823. [RGG#418]

MANN, ANTONY, from Ireland, graduated MD from Edinburgh University in 1785. [GME#18]

MANNIN, ANDREW, from Ireland, graduated MD from Edinburgh University in 1802. [GME#34]

MARK, WILLIAM, of Markston, Ireland, serviced as heir to his cousin John Alexander of Drummochreen, 24 April 1809. [NAS.S/H]

MARKEY, JAMES, from Ireland, graduated MD from Edinburgh University in 1798. [GME#28]

MARR, JOHN, second son of William Marr a farmer in the parish of Maghera, County Londonderry, matriculated at Glasgow University in 1794, graduated MA in 1797. [RGG#420]

MARSHAL, JOHN, graduated MA from Glasgow University in 1730, possibly a Presbyterian minister at Ballyclare. [RGG#420]

MARSHALL, FUTT, graduated MA from Glasgow University in 1776, a Presbyterian minister at Ballyclare, County Antrim, from 1785 to 1813, died 1813. [RGG#421]

MARSHALL, HUGH, from Ireland, graduated MA from Glasgow University in 1788. [RGG#421]

MARSHALL, JOHN, from Ireland, graduated MA from Glasgow University in 1767. [RGG#421]

MARSHALL, JOHN, graduated MA from Glasgow University in 1775, possibly the Presbyterian minister at Mayo. [RGG#420]

MARTIN, DAVID, youngest son of David Martin a farmer in the parish of Mullabrack, County Armagh, matriculated in 1818, graduated MA from Glasgow University in 1821. [RGG#423]

MARTIN, JAMES, eldest son of William Martin a farmer in the parish of Billey, County Antrim, matriculated in 1766, graduated MA from Glasgow University in 1770. [RGG#423]

MARTIN, JOHN, eldest son of Daniel Martin a farmer in the parish of Billy, County Antrim, matriculated in 1779, graduated MA from Glasgow University in 1781. [RGG#424]

MARTIN, JOHN GIBSON, from Ireland, graduated Ch.B. from Glasgow University in 1822. [RGG#424]

MARTIN, JOSEPH, eldest son of William Martin in the parish of Anaghlone, County Down, matriculated in 1807, graduated MA from Glasgow University in 1810. [RGG#424]

MARTIN, ROBERT, eldest son of James Martin in Dublin Castle, matriculated in 1759, graduated MA from Glasgow University in 1760. [RGG#424]

MARTIN, ROBERT, from Ireland, graduated CM from Glasgow University in 1818. [RGG#424]

MARTIN, WILLIAM, from Ireland, graduated MA from Glasgow University in 1776. [RGG#424]

MARTIN, WILLIAM KIRK, from Ireland, graduated CM from Glasgow University in 1819. [RGG#425]

MARTLEY, JAMES FREDERICK, from Ireland, graduated MD from Edinburgh University in 1782. [GME#16]

MATHEW, ROBERT, in Glenarm, was admitted as a burgess of Inveraray on 10 October 1733. [IBR]

MATTEAR, JOHN, from Ireland, graduated MD from Edinburgh University in 1749. [GME#4]

MAWE, THOMAS, from Ireland, graduated MD from Edinburgh University in 1803. [GME#34]

MAXWELL, WILLIAM, from Ireland, graduated MD from Edinburgh University in 1789. [GME#21]

MAYNE, HUGH, youngest son of John Mayne a farmer in
Saintfield, County Down, matriculated in 1811, graduated
MA from Glasgow University in 1815. [RGG#428]

MAYNE, JOSEPH, from Ireland, graduated MA from Glasgow
University in 1768. [RGG#428]

MAYWOOD, ROBERT, from Ireland, graduated MD from
Glasgow University in 1786. [RGG#428]

MEADE, WILLIAM, from Ireland, graduated MD from
Edinburgh University in 1790. [GME#22]

MEAGHER, JOHN, from Tipperaray, graduated MD from
Glasgow University in 1787. [RGG#429]

MEARS, JAMES, a merchant in Belfast, 1726.
[NAS.AC7/32/116-213]

MEASE, ANDREW, from Ireland, graduated MD from
Edinburgh University in 1777. [GME#13]

MECREDY, ALEXANDER, from Ireland, graduated MA from
Glasgow University in 1766. [RGG#429]

MEHARG, ARCHIBALD, graduated MA from Glasgow
University in 1800, an Irish Presbyterian minister at
Stonebridge from 1804 to 1849. [RGG#429]

MELVILL, ROBERT, eldest son of David Melvill a merchant
in Dublin, matriculated in 1788, graduated MA from
Glasgow University in 1791. [RGG#430]

MERCER, ALEXANDER, graduated DD from Glasgow
University in 1786, an Irish Presbyterian minister at
Dungannon from 1772 to 1776, then rector of an academy
near Dublin. [RGG#432]

MEYLER, ANTONY, from Ireland, graduated MD from
Edinburgh University in 1803. [GME#35]

MILES, JOHN, second son of John Miles of Rochestoun in the
parish of Ardfinnan, County Tipparary, matriculated at

Glasgow University in 1778, graduated MA in 1781. [RGG#433]

MILES, JOHN, from Ireland, graduated MA from Glasgow University in 1796. [RGG#433]

MILLER, JOSEPH, from Ireland, graduated MD from Edinburgh University in 1791. [GME#23]

MILLER, Miss ..., in Meikle Dunragit, Ireland, 1771, later in Philadelphia. [NAS.GD135.1649]

MILLET, EDWARD, from Ireland, graduated MD from Edinburgh University in 1795. [GME#26]

MILLIGAN, WILLIAM, from Ireland, graduated MD from Edinburgh University in 1822. [GME#68]

MILLS, THOMAS, from Ireland, graduated MD from Edinburgh University in 1797. [GME#27]

MINCHIN, BELINDA, daughter of Humphrey Minchin quartermaster of the Midlothian Fencibles, was buried in 1798. [Ballyhea parish register, Co. Cork]

MITCHELL, ANDREW, youngest son of Obadiah Mitchell in the parish of Maghera, County Londonderry, matriculated in 1814, graduated from Glasgow University in 1818. [RGG#440]

MITCHELL, THOMAS, second son of Thomas Mitchell a merchant in Ballymoney, County Antrim, matriculated in 1809, graduated MA from Glasgow University in 1812. [RGG#441]

MOAT, HENRY, son of Thomas Moat, of the Rothesay and Caithness Regiment, and his wife Mary, was baptised on 12 August 1798. [Cloyne Cathedral, Co. Cork]

MOFFETT, JAMES, second son of Samuel Moffett a merchant in the parish of Loughanisland, County Down, matriculated at Glasgow University in 1762, graduated MA in 1766. [RGG#443]

MOLLOY, JAMES, seond son of Charles Molloy in the parish
of Mucknow, County Monaghan, matriculated at Glasgow
University in 1764, graduated MA in 1766. [RGG#443]

MONRO, PHILADELPHIA JANE, daughter of Lt. Col.
Monro of the Caithness Legion, was baptised on 19 April
1800. [Ballymodan parish register, Co. Cork]

MONTGOMERY, GRIZEL, in Dublin, testament confirmed
with the Commissariat of Edinburgh on 23 January 1802.
[NAS.CC8.8.133/8]

MONTGOMERY, JOHN, in Newry, County Down, around
1773. [NAS.RS38.XIII.178]

MONTGOMERY, JOHN, graduated MA from Glasgow
University in 1818, an Irish Presbyterian minister at
Glenwherry from 1825 to 1869, died 22 July 1869.
[RGG#446]

MONTGOMERY, ROBERT, a merchant in Larne, was
admitted as a burgess of Inveraray on 17 July 1742. [IBR]

MONTGOMERY, ROBERT, mariner in Larne, former owner
of the Margaret of Larne, 1750. [NAS.CS16.1.84/41]

MONTGOMERY, ROBERT, from Ireland, graduated MD
from Edinburgh University in 1792. [GME#24]

MONTGOMERY, WILLIAM, a merchant in Larne, was
admitted as a burgess of Larne on 17 July 1742. [IBR]

MOODY, JAMES, from Ireland, graduated MD from
Edinburgh University in 1772. [GME#11]

MOODY, JOHN, eldest son of Reverend James Moody in
Newry, matriculated at Glasgow University in 1761,
graduated MA in 1764. [RGG#447]

MOORE, DAVID, second son of James Moore a farmer in the
parish of Aughabog, County Monaghan, matriculated at

Glasgow University in 1800, graduated MA in 1804. [RGG#447]

MOORE, HUGH, born 1804, graduated MA from Glasgow University in 1823, Unitarian minister at Newtonards, died 26 February 1893. [RGG#448]

MOORE, JAMES, fourth son of James Moore in County Antrim, matriculated at Glasgow University in 1761, graduated MA in 1763. [RGG#448]

MOORE, JOSEPH, from Ireland, graduated MD from Glasgow University in 1790. [RGG#448]

MOORE, MARSHALL, graduated MA from Glasgow University in 1816, an Irish Presbyterian minister at Faughanvale from 1819 to 1848, died 14 August 1848. [RGG#448]

MOORE, MATTHEW SCOTT, from Ireland, graduated MD from Edinburgh University in 1798. [GME#29]

MOORE, SAMUEL, from Ireland, graduated MD from Edinburgh University in 1778. [GME#14]

MOORE, SAMUEL, eldest son of William Moore a farmer in the parish of Kilmore, County Down, matriculated at Glasgow University in 1818, graduated MA in 1823. [RGG#449]

MOORE, WILLIAM, second son of Thomas Moore a farmer in the parish of Newtonards, County Down, matriculated at Glasgow University in 1816, graduated MA in 1818. [RGG#449]

MOORE, WILLIAM H., from Ireland, graduated CM from Glasgow University in 1822. [RGG#449]

MOORHEAD, JOHN NESBIT, graduated MD from Edinburgh University in 1821. [GME#65]

MORGAN, HILL, from Ireland, graduated MD from Edinburgh University in 1797. [GME#28]

MORGAN, JOHN, from Ireland, graduated MD from Edinburgh University in 1798. [GME#29]

MORIARTY, MERIONES M., graduated MD from Edinburgh University in 1821. [GME#65]

MORRISON, JAMES, from Ireland, graduated MA in 1766. [RGG#452]

MORRISON, JOHN, son of Hugh Morrison, of the Rothesay and Caithness Fencibles, and his wife Janet, was baptised on 23 February 1800. [Cloyne Cathedral, Co Cork]

MORROW, FRANCIS, eldest son of Thomas Morrow a wright in County Down, matriculated at Glasgow University in 1813, graduated MA in 1814. [RGG#453]

MORTON, JOHN, second son of Robert Morton a farmer in the parish of Knockbreda, County Down, matriculated at Glasgow University in 1816, graduated MA in 1819. [RGG#454]

MOUNTGARRET, JOHN, from Ireland, graduated MA from Glasgow University in 1764. [RGG#455]

MULHALLEN, WILLIAM, from Ireland, graduated MA from Glasgow University in 1766. [RGG#460]

MULLIGAN, HUGH, graduated MA from Glasgow University in 1737, an Irish Presbyterian minister at Bailieborough from 1742 to 1757, and at Aughnacloy from 1757 to 1786, died 1 January 1786. [RGG#460]

MUNDELL, SAMUEL, from Ireland, graduated MA from Glasgow University in 1793. [RGG#460]

MUNNS, GEORGE, graduated CM from Glasgow University in 1819, in Holywell, County Leitrim, later in Oxford, Ohio. [RGG#461]

MUNNS, JOHN, second son of Reverend Edward Munns, Archdeacon of the Diocese of Elphin and minister of the

parish of Drumclife, County Sligo, matriculated at
Glasgow University in 1747, graduated MA in 1749.
[RGG#461]

MURDOCH, ROBERT, from Ireland, graduated MD from
Edinburgh University in 1754. [GME#6]

MURPHY, JOHN, from Ireland, graduated MD from
Edinburgh University in 1782. [GME#16]

MURPHY, PATRICK, graduated MD from Edinburgh
University in 1821. [GME#65]

MURPHY, WILLIAM, eldest son of William Murphy a farmer
in the parish of Drumballyrony, County Down,
matriculated at Glasgow University in 1817, graduated
MA in 1821. [RGG#463]

MURRAY, ANN, a widow from Charleston, South Carolina,
settled in Doneraile, County Cork, 1763.
[NAS.GD219.285]

MURRAY, FRANCIS, from Ireland, graduated MD from
Glasgow University in 1820. [RGG#463]

MURRELL, JAMES, from Ireland, graduated MA from
Glasgow University in 1794. [RGG#465]

NAGHTON, TIMOTHY, from Ireland, graduated MD from
Edinburgh University in 1804. [GME#35]

NEILSON, MOSES, graduated MA in 1763 and DD in 1792
from the University of Glasgow, a Presbyterian minister at
Kilmore, County Down, from 1767 to 1823, died 23 April
1823. [RGG#468]

NEILSON, SAMUEL, second son of James Neilson a farmer in
the parish of Cumber, County Down, matriculated at
Glasgow University in 1813, graduated MA in 1816.
[RGG#468]

NEILSON, WILLIAM, born 12 September 1774, son of
Reverend Moses Neilson in Kilmore, County Down, a

Presbyterian minister at Dundalk from 1796 to 1818 and
Rector of the Academy there, then Professor of Classics at
the Belfast Academical Institution, graduated DD from
Glasgow University in 1805, died 27 April 1821.
[RGG#468]

NEILSON, WILLIAM, eldest son of John Neilson a farmer in
the parish of Termanneny, County Londonderry,
matriculated at Glasgow University in 1814, graduated
MA in 1818. [RGG#468]

NELSON, JAMES, born 1 May 1768, graduated MA in 1788
and DD in 1817 from Glasgow University, minister of the
Presbyterian congregation in Downpatrick from 1791 to
1838, died 28 January 1838. [RGG#469]

NELSON, SAMUEL CRAIG, graduated MA from Glasgow
University in 1823, a Presbyterian minister at
Downpatrick. [RGG#469]

NESBIT, JOHN, of Woodhill, 1746. [NAS.GD10.948]

NESBITT, WILLIAM, of Drimance, County Donegal, 1746.
[NAS.GD10.947]

NEVIN, WILLIAM, an Irish Presbyterian minister at
Downpatrick from 1785 to 1789, graduated MD from
Glasgow University in 1794. [RGG#469]

NEWALL, WILLIAM in Belfast, 1798. [NAS.GD307.16.4]

NEWENHAM, HENRY, from Ireland, graduated MD from
Edinburgh University in 1822. [GME#68]

NEWMAN, CHARLES, from Ireland, graduated MD from
Edinburgh University in 1773. [GME#11]

NEWSOM, HENRY, eldest son of Moses Newsom a merchant
in Cork, matriculated at Glasgow University in 1762,
graduated MA in 1763. [RGG#470]

NIBLOCK, JAMES, from Ireland, graduated MD from
Edinburgh University in 1800. [GME#31]

NICHOLSON, ADAM, soldier of the Rothesay and Caithness Fencibles, married Mary Meade on 12 September 1798. [Cloyne Cathedral, Co. Cork]

NICHOLSON, JOHN, from Ireland, graduated MD from Glasgow University in 1812. [RGG#471]

NIHILL, JOHN, from Killahoe, County Clare, graduated CM from Glasgow University in 1825. [RGG#472]

NISBET, RICHARD, eldest son of John Nisbet a farmer in the parish of Donagheady, County Tyrone, matriculated at Glasgow University in 1769, graduated MA in 1770. [RGG#473]

NIXON, GEORGE, eldest son of Reverend Andrew Nixon rector of the parish of Ana, County Cavan, matriculated at Glasgow University in 1772, graduated MA in 1774. [RGG#473]

NIXON, MONTGOMERY, from Ireland, graduated MD from Edinburgh University in 1789. [GME#21]

NUGENT, EDWARD, from Ireland, graduated MD from Edinburgh University in 1780. [GME#15]

O'BEIRN, BRYAN, from Ireland, graduated MD from Edinburgh University in 1803. [GME#35]

O'BRENAN, JOHN, from Ireland, graduated MD from Glasgow University in 1802. [RGG#474]

O'BRIEN, MATTHEW, from Ireland, graduated MD from Edinburgh University in 1801. [GME#32]

O'CALLAGHAN, DAVID, from Ireland, graduated MD from Edinburgh University in 1800. [GME#31]

O'CONNELL, DENNIS, from Ireland, graduated MD from Glasgow University in 1825. [RGG#475]

O'CONNELL, GALFRID, from Ireland, graduated MD from Edinburgh University in 1766. [GME#9]

O'CONNOR, ARTHUR JAMES, from Ireland, graduated MD from Edinburgh University in 1794. [GME#25]

O'CONNOR, EDMUND, from Ireland, graduated MA from Glasgow University in 1791. [RGG#475]

O'CONNOR, JAMES, from Ireland, graduated MA from Glasgow University in 1779. [RGG#475]

O'DONOGHUE, HUGH, from Ireland, graduated CM from Glasgow University in 1820. [RGG#475]

O'DWYER, WILLIAM, graduated MD from Glasgow University in 1784, staff physician, Army Medical Department, Ireland. [RGG#475]

O'FERRALL, HUGH, from Ireland, graduated MD from Glasgow University in 1788. [RGG#475]

OGILBY, ROBERT, from Ireland, graduated MD from Edinburgh University in 1756. [GME#6]

O'HALLORAN, WILLIAM SAUNDERS, from Ireland, graduated MD from Edinburgh University in 1788. [GME#20]

O'HEA, STANDISH, from Ireland, graduated MD from Edinburgh University in 1797. [GME#27]

O'KAINE, EALIN, a harper from Coleraine, County Londonderry, was admitted as a burgess of Inveraray on 9 September 1751. [IBR]

O'LEARY, PHILIP, from Ireland, graduated MD from Edinburgh University in 1822. [GME#68]

OLIVER, ANDREW, eldest son of Thomas Oliver in the parish of Enniskillen, County Fermanagh, matriculated at Glasgow University in 1769, graduated MA in 1771. [RGG#476]

O'MEAGHER, THOMAS, from Ireland, graduated MD from Edinburgh University in 1795. [GME#26]

O'MEAGHER, WILLIAM, from Ireland, graduated MD at Glasgow University in 1791. [RGG#477]

O'NEIL, CHARLES, second son of John O'Neil a gentleman in the parish of Ray, County Donegal, matriculated at Glasgow University in 1779, graduated MA in 1780. [RGG#477]

O'NEIL, WILLIAM, from Ireland, graduated MD from Glasgow University in 1791. [RGG#477]

O'NEILL, CLOTWORTHY, graduated MA from Glasgow University in 1736, High Sheriff of County Antrim. [RGG#477]

O'NEILL, CONOLLY, third son of Reverend James O'Neill minister of the parish of Kilbarren, County Donegal, matriculated at Glasgow University in 1774, graduated MA in 1776. [RGG#477]

O'NEILL, HUGH, from Ireland, graduated CM from Glasgow University in 1821. [RGG#477]

O'NEILL, MARKER, son of Felix O'Neill a gentleman in County Antrim, matriculated at Glasgow University in 1733, graduated MA in 1735. [RGG#477]

O'REARDON, JOHN, from Ireland, graduated MD from Edinburgh University in 1802. [GME#33]

O'REDY, JAMES, from Ireland, graduated MD from Glasgow University in 1785. [RGG#477]

O'REGAN, JOHN, from Ireland, graduated MD from Edinburgh University in 1822. [GME#68]

O'REILLY, EDWARD, from Ireland, graduated MD from Glasgow University in 1818. [RGG#477]

ORMSBY, CALDWELL, from Ireland, graduated MD from Edinburgh University in 1821. [GME#65]

ORPEN, JOHN HEDRBERT, from Ireland, graduated MD from Edinburgh University in 1763. [GME#8]

ORPEN, THOMAS HERBERT, from Ireland, graduated MD from Edinburgh University in 1797. [GME#28]

ORR, JAMES, from Ireland, graduated MD from Edinburgh University in 1821. [GME#65]

ORR, JOHN, the Archdeacon of Ferns, Ireland, graduated as a Doctor of Divinity from Edinburgh University on 26 April 1763. [CEG#243]

ORR, JOHN, graduated MA from Glasgow University in 1815, a Presbyterian minister at Portaferry, County Down, from 1822 to 1878, died 4 November 1878. [RGG#478]

ORR, ROBERT, second son of Alexander Orr a merchant in Belford, County Antrim, matriculated at Glasgow University in 1813, graduated MA in 1816. [RGG#479]

O'RYAN, JOHN, graduated MD from Glasgow University in 1791, settled in Waterford. [RGG#479]

O'RYAN, PATRICK, from Ireland, graduated MD from Edinburgh University in 1822. [GME#68]

OSBORNE, GEORGE, from Ireland, graduated MD from Edinburgh University in 1801. [GME#32]

O'SULLIVAN, THOMAS, from Ireland, graduated MD from Edinburgh University in 1799. [GME#30]

OSWALD, or BUCHANAN, ANN, relict of John, Lord Bishop of Raphoe, Ireland, 1781. [NAS.RS.Fife#11]

PAINE, JOSEPH, Anglo-Irish, son of Laurence Paine of Navan, a gentleman in County Meath, matriculated at Glasgow University in 1732, graduated MA in 1734, and DD in 1764. [RGG#481]

PARK, ROBERT, graduated MA from Glasgow University in 1812, an Irish Presbyterian minister at Ballymoney from 1817 to 1876. [RGG#482]

PARKE, JOHN, from Ireland, graduated MD from Edinburgh University in 1821. [GME#65]

PARKER, MICHAEL, from Ireland, graduated MD from Edinburgh University in 1794. [GME#25]

PARKER, PATRICK, eldest son of Samuel Parker a merchant in Tandragee town, County Armagh, matriculated at Glasgow University in 1768, graduated MA in 1770. [RGG#483]

PATERSON, ANDREW, Scots-Irish, graduated MA from Glasgow University in 1771. [RGG#485]

PATERSON, JAMES, graduated MA from Glasgow University in 1780, possibly an Irish Presbyterian minister at Ardglass from 1772 to 1898, died 7 May 1798. [RGG#483]

PATRICK, ELIZABETH, daughter of Benjamin and Isabella Patrick, was baptised on 18 August 1799. [St Nicholas parish register, Cork]

PATRICK, JAMES, son of William, a corporal of the Rothesay and Caithness Regiment, and his wife Jane, was baptised on 19 August 1798. [Cloyne Cathedral, Co. Cork]

PATTEN, FRANCIS, youngest son of Reverend William Patten in Dublin, matriculated at Glasgow University in 1763, graduated MA in 1766. [RGG#490]

PATTEN, SAMUEL, graduated MA from Glasgow University in 1764, possibly an Irish Presbyterian minister. [RGG#490]

PATTERSON, JAMES, eldest son of Samuel Patterson a farmer in the parish of Desmartin, County Londonderry,

matriculated in 1808, graduated MA from Glasgow
University in 1811. [RGG#491]

PATTERSON, JAMES PARKER, from Ireland, graduated
CM from Glasgow University in 1823. [RGG#491]

PATTERSON, JOHN, second son of William Patterson a
farmer in the parish of Boho, County Fermanagh,
matriculated at Glasgow University in 1772, graduated
MA in 1774. [RGG#491]

PATTERSON, JOHN, graduated MA from Glasgow
University in 1811, possibly an Irish Presbyterian minister
at Macosquin from 1817 to 1822. [RGG#491]

PATTERSON, TRISTRAM, third son of William Patterson in
Rathmelton, County Donegal, matriculated at Glasgow
University in 1774, graduated MA in 1776. [RGG#491]

PATTERSON, WILLIAM, graduated MA, MD, from Glasgow
University in 1772, possibly later in Londonderry.
[RGG#491]

PATTON, NATHAN, eldest son of Nathan Patton a farmer in
County Donegal, matriculated at Glasgow University in
1779, graduated MA in 1781. [RGG#492]

PELISSIER, ALEXANDER, from Ireland, graduated MD from
Edinburgh University in 1784. [GME#17]

PENTLAND, JOHN, from Ireland, graduated MD from
Edinburgh University in 1789. [GME#21]

PERCIVAL, ROBERT, from Ireland, graduated MD from
Edinburgh University in 1780. [GME#15]

PERSSE, WILLIAM, eldest son of Patrick Persse in County
Galway, matriculated at Glasgow University in 1771,
graduated MA in 1772. [RGG#495]

PHELAN, PERSES, from Ireland, graduated MD from
Edinburgh University in 1798. [GME#28]

PLUNKETT, PATRICK, from Ireland, graduated MD from Edinburgh University in 1779. [GME#15]

POLLOCK, JAMES, from Ireland, graduated MA from Glasgow University in 1769. [RGG#498]

POLLOCK, JOSEPH, eldest son of James Pollock a gentleman in Ballyedmond, County Down, matriculated at Glasgow University in 1767, graduated MA in 1769. [RGG#499]

PORTER, JAMES, third son of Hugh Porter a farmer in the parish of Monaghan, County Monaghan, matriculated at Glasgow University in 1801, graduated MA in 1805. [RGG#500]

PORTER, JAMES, eldest son of John Porter a farmer in Tullylune, County Monaghan, matriculated at Glasgow University in 1805, graduated MA in 1807. [RGG#500]

PORTER, WILLIAM, graduated MA from Glasgow University in 1795, an Irish Presbyterian minister at Newtown Limavady from 1799. [RGG#501]

POWELL, NATHANIEL, from Ireland, graduated MD from Edinburgh University in 1798. [GME#29]

POWER, GERARD, from Ireland, graduated MD from Glasgow University in 1785. [RGG#501]

POWER, JOHN, from Ireland, graduated MD from Glasgow University in 1812. [RGG#501]

PRENDERGAST, JOHN, from Ireland, graduated MD from Edinburgh University in 1786. [GME#19]

PRENTER, EDWARD, eldest son of Thomas Prenter a farmer in the parish of Dromore, County Down, matriculated at Glasgow University in 1805, graduated MA in 1809. [RGG#501]

PROSSER, JAMES, from Ireland, graduated MD from Edinburgh University in 1777. [GME#13]

PURDON, ROWAN, from Ireland, graduated MD from
Edinburgh University in 1799. [GME#30]

PURSS, JAMES, graduated MA from Glasgow University in
1812, minister of the Irish Presbyterian congregation of
Urney and Sion from 1824 to 1836, died 29 August 1836.
[RGG#504]

PYNE, CORNELIUS, from Ireland, graduated MD from
Edinburgh University in 1785. [GME#18]

QUIN, CHARLES WILLIAM, from Ireland, graduated MD
from Edinburgh University in 1779. [GME#15]

QUIN, O'NEIL, from Ireland, graduated MD from Edinburgh
University in 1822. [GME#68]

RADCLIFF, THOMAS, from Ireland, graduated MA from
Glasgow University in 1786. [RGG#505]

RAFFERTY, WILLIAM, from Ireland, graduated MA from
Glasgow University in 1800. [RGG#505]

RAINEY, ROBERT, son of Francis Rainey MD in Newry,
County Down, matriculated in 1755, graduated MA from
Glasgow University in 1758. [RGG#505]

RAINEY, WILLIAM, only son of Robert Rainey a merchant in
Newry, matriculated at Glasgow University in 1766,
graduated MA in 1771. [RGG#506]

RALSTON, THOMAS, from Ireland, graduated MA from
Glasgow University in 1771. [RGG#506]

RAMSAY. JOHN, fourth son of Reverend William Ramsay in
the parish of Raphoe, County Donegal, matriculated at
Glasgow University in 1818, graduated MA in 1821.
[RGG#507]

RAYMOND, SAMUEL, from Ireland, graduated MD from
Edinburgh University in 1821. [GME#66]

READE, JOSEPH, from Ireland, graduated MD from Edinburgh University in 1802. [GME#34]

REAH, JOSEPH, graduated MA from Glasgow University in 1742, an Irish Presbyterian minister at Fahan from 1748 to 1770, then emigrated to America. [RGG#510]

REARDON, SIMON, from Ireland, graduated MD from Edinburgh University in 1797. [GME#28]

REDMAN, SAMUEL, son of Reverend Samuel Redman in the parish of Kilmore, County Down, matriculated at Glasgow University in 1735, graduated MA in 1738. [RGG#510]

REED, HENRY, graduated MA, MD, from Glasgow University in 1772, possibly of the Army Medical Department in Ireland in 1797. [RGG#511]

REID, ALEXANDER, formerly in Coupar Angus, Perthshire, afterwards in Ireland, confirmation of testament 21 January 1789 Commissariat of Edinburgh.

REID, DAVID, graduated MA from Glasgow University in 1808, possibly an Irish Presbyterian minister at Dunfanaghy from 1830 to 1860, died 11 July 1860. [RGG#511]

REID, THOMAS, third son of David Reid a farmer in the parish of Killinchy, County Down, matriculated at Glasgow University in 1814, graduated MA in 1817. [RGG#514]

REID, THOMAS MAYNE, born 1787, graduated MA from Glasgow University in 1804, a Presbyterian minister in Drumgooland, presbytery of Rathfriland, died 9 July 1868. [RGG#514]

REIKY, ROBERT, in Dublin, testament confirmed with the Commissariat of Edinburgh on 6 June 1822. [NAS.CC8.8.148/134]

REILLY, MATTHEW, a soldier of the Caithness Legion, married Catherine Mahoney, on 8 September 1799. [Ballymodan parish register, Co. Cork]

RENDALL, JOHN, Examiner of the Customs at Dublin, 1754. [NAS.RS27.144.151]

REYNETT, HENRY, A.B., Vicar of Billy, Ireland, graduated as a Doctor of Divinity from Edinburgh University on 20 November 1793. [CEG#247]

REYNOLDS, HEWITSON, eldest son of John Reynolds a gentleman in the parish of Kilbarran, County Donegal, graduated MA from Glasgow University in 1777. [RGG#516]

REYNOLDS, JAMES, from Ireland, graduated MD from Edinburgh University in 1787. [GME#20]

RICHARDSON, GILBRAITH, from Ireland, graduated from Edinburgh University on 22 March 1733. [CEG#205]

RIDDELL, ROBERT, from Ireland, graduated CM from Glasgow University in 1825. [RGG#518]

ROBINSON, JAMES TEMPLETON, from Ireland, graduated MA, MD, from Glasgow University in 1784. [RGG#526]

ROBINSON, JOHN, second son of James Robinson a merchant in Markethill, County Armagh, matriculated at Glasgow University in 1768, graduated MA in 1770. [RGG#526]

ROBINSON, RICHARD, from Ireland, graduated MD from Edinburgh University in 1821. [GME#66]

RODGERS, ANDREW, sixth son of James Rodgers a merchant in the parish of Kildalan, County Cavan, matriculated at Glasgow University in 1771, graduated MA in 1774. [RGG#528]

RODGERS, MOSES, graduated MA from Glasgow University in 1821, intended for the Irish Presbyterian Church but emigrated to the United States and died there in the 1860s. [RGG#528]

ROE, EDWARD, from Ireland, graduated MA from Glasgow University in 1774. [RGG#528]

ROE, GEORGE, from Ireland, graduated MD from Edinburgh University in 1821. [GME#66]

ROGERS, BAYLEY, from Ireland, graduated MD from Edinburgh University in 1749. [GME#4]

ROGERS, CHRISTOPHER, from Ireland, graduated MD from Edinburgh University in 1751. [GME#4]

ROGERS, DAVID, graduated MA from Glasgow University in 1814, possibly an Irish Presbyterian minister at Killala from 1820 to 1859, died in June 1859. [RGG#528]

ROGERS, JOHN, graduated MA from Glasgow University in 1764, minister at Ballibay alias Cahans in 1767, Professor of Divinity to the Irish Burgher Synod from 1796 to 1814, died 24 August 1814. [RGG#528]

ROGERS, JOHN, son of John Rogers MA, graduated MA from Glasgow University in 1794, a Presbyterian minister at Glascar from 1798 to 1854, died on 25 December 1854. [RGG#529]

ROGERS, JOSEPH, from Ireland, graduated MD from Edinburgh University in 1778. [GME#14]

ROGERS, NATHAN, eldest son of William Rogers a farmer in the parish of Taughboyne, County Donegal, matriculated at Glasgow University in 1807, graduated MA in 1810. [RGG#529]

ROGERS, QUINTIN, son of Christopher Rogers a gentleman and lawyer in Mountpleasant, County Cork, matriculated at Glasgow University in 1743, graduated MA in 1750. [RGG#529]

ROME, JANE, daughter of Peter and Mary Rome from
Berwickshire, was baptised on 2 December 1798. [St
Nicholas parish register, Cork]

ROSE, GEORGE, eldest son of Thomas Rose a gentleman in
County Limerick, matriculated at Glasgow University in
1765, graduated MA in 1766. [RGG#530]

ROSE, JOHN, from Ireland, graduated MA in 1769.
[RGG#530]

ROSS, ALEXANDER, from Ireland, graduated MD from
Edinburgh University in 1754. [GME#5]

ROSS, CATHERINE, daughter of Thomas Ross, of the
Rothesay and Caithness Regiment, and his wife Janet, was
baptised on 9 March 1800. [Cloyne Cathedral, Co. Cork]

ROSS, DAVID, 'Scots-Irish', matriculated at Glasgow
University in 1727, graduated MA in 1728. [RGG#531]

ROSS, RICHARD, fourth son of David Ross a merchant in the
parish of Monaghan, County Monaghan, matriculated at
Glasgow University in 1802, graduated MA in 1806.
[RGG#532]

ROWAN, JAMES, son of Reverend John Rowan in County
Down, matriculated at Glasgow University in 1739,
graduated MA in 1739. [RGG#533]

ROWLAND, WILLIAM, eldest son of William Rowland an
army officer in County Cork, matriculated at Glasgow
University in 17755, graduated MA in 1758. [RGG#533]

ROWLAND, WILLIAM, from Ireland, graduated MD from
Edinburgh University in 1763. [GME#8]

RUNCIE, JAMES, second son of John Runcie a farmer in the
parish of Cregan, County Armagh, matriculated at
Glasgow University in 1772, graduated MA in 1773.
[RGG#534]

RUSSELL, ALEXANDER, in Kilkenny, 1787.
[NAS.GD216.225]

RUSSELL, WILLIAM THOMAS, from Ireland, graduated
MD from Edinburgh University in 1800. [GME#32]

RUTHERFORD, JOHN, third son of Reverend Samuel
Rutherford in the parish of Killevan, County Monaghan,
matriculated at Glasgow University in 1792, graduated
MA in 1795. [RGG#537]

RUTHERFORD, WILLIAM, graduated CM from Glasgow
University in 1824, in Annahilt, County Down, died in
June 1866. [RGG#538]

RYAN, JAMES, from Ireland, graduated MD from Edinburgh
University in 1803. [GME#35]

RYAN, JEREMY, from Ireland, graduated MD from
Edinburgh University in 1800. [GME#32]

RYAN, MICHAEL, from Ireland, graduated MD from
Edinburgh University in 1784. [GME#17]

RYAN, MICHAEL, from Ireland, graduated MD from
Edinburgh University in 1821. [GME#66]

RYAN, RICHARD, from Ireland, graduated MD from
Edinburgh University in 1799. [GME#30]

RYAN, THOMAS, from Ireland, graduated MD from
Edinburgh University in 1784. [GME#17]

RYLAND, WILLIAM NEWCOMBE, from Ireland, graduated
MD from Glasgow University in 1825. [RGG#538]

SANDILAND, GEORGE, in Carrickfergus, 1797.
[NAS.GD7.2.87]

SAUNDERS, WILLIAM, from Ireland, graduated MD from
Edinburgh University in 1802. [GME#33]

SAYERS, ANDREW, from Ireland, graduated MD from Edinburgh University in 1782. [GME#16]

SAYERS, WILLIAM LYSAGHT, from Ireland, graduated MD from Edinburgh University in 1800. [GME#31]

SCANLAN, JOHN, from Ireland, graduated MD from Edinburgh University in 1751. [GME#4]

SCOTT, JAMES, from Ireland, graduated MD from Edinburgh University in 1795. [GME#26]

SCOTT, ROBERT, from Ireland, graduated MD from Edinburgh University in 1778. [GME#14]

SCOTT, ROBERT, in Belfast, 1798. [NAS.AC7/71]

SCOTT, UPTON, born in Ireland during 1722, a physician educated at Glasgow University, graduated MD in 1753, and possibly in Edinburgh, settled in Maryland, died 1814. [SA#178]

SCOTT, WILLIAM, in Dublin, 1770. [NAS.CS16.1.138]

SCOTT, WILLIAM, from Ireland, graduated MD from Edinburgh University in 1786. [GME#18]

SCOTT, WILLIAM, Judge of King's Bench, Ireland, 1773. [NAS.CS16.1.154/156]

SCULLY, WILLIAM, from Ireland, graduated MD from Edinburgh University in 1801. [GME#32]

SEMPLE, WILLIAM, from Ireland, graduated MD from Edinburgh University in 1751. [GME#5]

SHADWELL, THOMAS, from Ireland, graduated MD from Edinburgh University in 1779. [GME#15]

SHAFTON, BENJAMIN, from Ireland, graduated MD from Edinburgh University in 1751. [GME#5]

SHARP, THOMAS, from Ireland, graduated MD from
Edinburgh University in 1794. [GME#25]

SHEA, WILLIAM JOHN, from Ireland, graduated MD from
Edinburgh University in 1798. [GME#29]

SHEEHY, JOHN, from Ireland, graduated MD from Edinburgh
University in 1796. [GME#27]

SHERLOCK, JOSEPH, from Ireland, graduated MD from
Edinburgh University in 1788. [GME#21]

SHERRARD, WILLIAM SHIRDON, a soldier of the
Caithness Legion, was buried 16 December 1796.
[Ballyhea parish register, Co. Cork]

SHIEL, JOHN BARCLAY, from Ireland, graduated MD from
Edinburgh University in 1821. [GME#66]

SHIELL, HUGH, from Ireland, graduated MD from Edinburgh
University in 1765. [GME#8]

SHIELLS, JAMES, from Ireland, graduated MD from
Edinburgh University in 1822. [GME#68]

SHUTER, JAMES, from Ireland, graduated MD from
Edinburgh University in 1800. [GME#32]

SIMPSON, JOHN, from Ireland, graduated MD from
Edinburgh University in 1787. [GME#19]

SINCLAIR, ALEXANDER, from Ireland graduated MD from
Edinburgh University in 1822. [GME#69]

SINCLAIR, JOHN, son of Charles Sinclair a soldier of the
Caithness Legion, was baptised on 10 November 1799.
[Ballymodan parish register, Co. Cork]

SINCLAIR, ELINOR and BARBARA, twin daughters of John
Sinclair of the Caithness Legion, were baptised on 1
February 1800. [Ballymodan parish register, Co. Cork]

SINCLAIR, WILLIAM, from Ireland, graduated MD from
Edinburgh University in 1822. [GME#69]

SINKLER, ANGUS, a merchant in Belfast, was admitted as a
burgess of Inveraray on 7 October 1754. [IBR]

SKELTON, FRANCIS, from Ireland, graduated MD from
Edinburgh University in 1759. [GME#7]

SKELTON, WILLIAM, from Ireland, graduated from
Edinburgh University on 2 March 1736. [CEG#206]

SLACKE, RANDAL JAMES, from Ireland, graduated MD
from Edinburgh University in 1794. [GME#25]

SLEIGH, JOSEPH FENN, from Ireland, graduated MD from
Edinburgh University in 1753. [GME#5]

SMALL, SARAH, in Coleraine, County Londonderry,
testament confirmed with the Commissariat of Edinburgh
on 4 September 1829. [NAS.CC8.8.152/166]

SMART, ALEXANDER, a soldier of the Caithness Legion,
married Catherine Neagle on 8 September 1799.
[Ballymodan parish register, Co. Cork]

SMEATON, HELEN, daughter of John Smeaton, sergeant of
the Rothesay and Caithness Regiment, and his wife Janet,
was baptised on 5 August 1796. [Cloyne Cathedral
register, Cork]

SMITH, BERNARD, pilot of Youghal, 1730. [NAS.AC9.1116]

SMITH, DONALD, in Wicklow, 1795. [NAS.GD13.231]

SMITH, JAMES, from Ireland, graduated from the University
of Edinburgh on 4 February 1732. [CEG#204]

SMITH, JOHN, from Ireland, graduated MD from Edinburgh
University in 1794. [GME#25]

SMITHWICK, PETER, from Ireland, graduated MD from
Edinburgh University in 1822. [GME#69]

SMITHWICK, ROBERT, from Ireland, graduated MD from Edinburgh University in 1787. [GME#20]

SMYTH, WILLIAM HAMILTON, from Ireland, graduated MD from Edinburgh University in 1801. [GME#33]

SOMERS, EDMUND, from Ireland, graduated MD from Edinburgh University in 1783. [GME#17]

SPROUL, JOHN, sometime student of medicine at Edinburgh University then a physician in Dublin, husband of Jean, daughter of James Millar a writer in Selkirk, process of Divorce, 1785. [Commissariat of Edinburgh]

SPROULE, JOHN WATSON, from Ireland, graduated MD from Edinburgh University in 1787. [GME#19]

STARK, JAMES CHARLES, in Carlow, testament confirmed with the Commissariat of Edinburgh on 4 June 1824. [NAS.CC8.8.150/183]

STARRAT, JOHN, from Ireland, graduated MD from Edinburgh University in 17490. [GME#22]

STEPHENSON, SAMUEL MARTIN, from Ireland, graduated MD from Edinburgh University in 1776. [GME#13]

STEVENSON, HENRY, born in Ireland during 1721, a physician educated in Ireland, England and Scotland, settled in Maryland, died 1814. [SA#178]

STEVENSON, WILLIAM, from Ireland, graduated MD from Edinburgh University in 1762. [GME#7]

STEWART, GEORGE, of the Royal Hospital, Dublin, 1808. [NAS.GD13.368]

STEWART, JOHN, from Ireland, graduated MD from Edinburgh University in 1794. [GME#25]

STEWART, RANDOLPH SMYTH, from Ireland, graduated MD from Edinburgh University in 1821. [GME#66]

STEWART, WILLIAM, a merchant in Ayr, then in Cork by 1813. [NAS.CS17.1.32/311]

STILL, ALEXANDER, a minister in Tulliclay, Ireland, serviced as heir to his uncle George Still an embroiderer in Canongate, Edinburgh, on 21 February 1727. [NAS.SH]

STOKER, WILLIAM, from Ireland, graduated MD from Edinburgh University in 1798. [GME#29]

STOKES, WILLIAM, from Ireland, graduated MD from Edinburgh University in 1797. [GME#28]

STREAN, ANNESLEY, from Ireland, graduated MD from Edinburgh University in 1790. [GME#22]

SWAN, DOUGAL, son of George Swan of the Berwick Fencible Horse, was baptised on 6 December 1799. [Ballymodan parish register, Co. Cork]

SWEET, JOHN, of Pleasantfield, Ireland, 1783. [NAS.RS.Fife#749]

SWIFT, JOHN, from Ireland, graduated MD from Edinburgh University in 1800. [GME#31]

TATE, RICHARD, from Ireland, graduated MD from Edinburgh University in 1822. [GME#69]

TAYLOR, CHARLES, in 1801. [NAS.GD1.120.21]

THOM, JOHN, born in Aberdeen during 1776, son of John Thom, educated at King's College, Aberdeen, graduated MA on 29 March 1798, licentiate of the Presbytery of Auchterarder, ordained a minister at Newry on 5 August 1800, died on 18 July 1808. [F.7.533]

THOMAS, BARTHOLEMEW, from Ireland, graduated MD from Edinburgh University in 1775. [GME#12]

THOMSON, ARTHUR, son of late James Thomson a
merchant in Belfast, 1775. [NAS.CS16.1.165/163]

THOMSON, BENJAMIN, from Ireland, graduated MD from
Edinburgh University in 1822. [GME#69]

THOMSON, JAMES, a merchant in Belfast, 1775.
[NAS.CS16.1.165/173]

THOMSON, JOHN, son of Hugh Thomson a merchant and
sailor in Coleraine, County Antrim, heir of Hugh
Thomson in Irvine, 1728. [NAS.GD1.693.22]

THOMSON, SAMUEL SMITH, from Ireland, graduated MD
from Edinburgh University in 1800. [GME#31]

THOMSON, WILLIAM, a shoemaker in Dumfries, then in
Doneraile, County Cork, dead by 1763.
[NAS.GD219.286]

TILLER, ROBERT, soldier of the Caithness Highlanders,
married Ellen Mahoney on 29 May 1800. [Cloyne
Cathedral, Co. Cork]

TOWNSEND, EDWARD, from Ireland, graduated MD from
Edinburgh University in 1822. [GME#69]

TOWNSEND, RICHARD, from Ireland, graduated MD from
Edinburgh University in 1759. [GME#7]

TOWNSEND, THOMAS, a barrister in Dublin, graduated as a
Doctor of Law at Edinburgh University on 20 March
1808. [CEG#260]

TRAVERS, PATRICK, from Ireland, graduated MD from
Edinburgh University in 1822. [GME#69]

TROWTON, LEONARD, son of John Trowton of the
Rothesay and Caithness Fencibles, was baptised on 13
January 1799. [Cloyne Cathedral, Co.Cork]

TUCKEY, THOMAS, from Ireland, graduated MD from
Edinburgh University in 1798. [GME#29]

TURNER, WILLIAM HENRY, from Ireland, graduated MD from Edinburgh University in 1798. [GME#29]

UNTHANK, ISAAC, from Ireland, graduated MD from Edinburgh University in 1748. [GME#4]

UNTHANK, ISAAC, from Ireland, graduated MD from Edinburgh University in 1803. [GME#34]

UNTHANK, JONATHAN, from Ireland, graduated MD from Edinburgh University in 1784. [GME#17]

USSHER, JOHN, from Ireland, graduated MD from Edinburgh University in 1785. [GME#18]

VENABLES, PETER, from Ireland, graduated MD from Edinburgh University in 1803. [GME#34]

VIZE, JOHN, from Ireland, graduated MD from Edinburgh University in 1778. [GME#14]

WADE, BRYAN, from Ireland, graduated MD from Edinburgh University in 1755. [GME#6]

WAINWRIGHT, JAMES, from Ireland, graduated MD from Edinburgh University in 1755. [GME#6]

WALLACE, JOHN, a merchant in Killyleagh, County Down, husband of Jean, daughter of Fergus Lyon of Little Larg and Katherine McCubbin, 1762. [NAS.GD135.959]

WALLACE, PETER, born 1788, son of Daniel Wallace and Janet Jamieson, died 13 March 1818, buried in St Mark's, Dublin. [Kirkmaiden gravestone, Wigtownshire]

WALLACE, THOMAS, from Ireland, graduated MD from Edinburgh University in 1787. [GME#20]

WALSH, LAURENCE, from Ireland, graduated MD from Edinburgh University in 1784. [GME#18]

WALSH, PHILIP P., from Ireland, graduated MD from Edinburgh University in 1780. [GME#15]

WARE, SUSANNA, in Belfast, 1818. [NAS.GD154.687/1]

WARREN, EBENEZER, from Ireland, graduated MD from Edinburgh University in 1794. [GME#25]

WARREN, JOHN, soldier of the Caithness Legion, married Mary Riordan on 16 July 1799. [Ballymodan parish register, Co. Cork]

WATSON, JOHN, WALDRON, from Ireland, graduated MD from Edinburgh University in 1822. [GME#69]

WELD, ISAAC, A.M., Dublin, graduated as a Doctor of Divinity from Edinburgh University on 26 February 1766. [CEG#243]

WEST, JOHN, in Dublin, 1789. [NAS.GD216.229]

WEST, WILLIAM, from Ireland, graduated MD from Edinburgh University in 1821. [GME#66]

WESTROP, THOMAS, from Ireland, graduated MD from Edinburgh University in 1779. [GME#15]

WHEELER, Reverend OLIVER, Mountbrilliant, Kilkenny, 1771. [NAS.GD155/467]

WHITE, JOHN, from Ireland, graduated from Edinburgh University on 14 February 1738. [CEG#207]

WHITELAW, WILLIAM, from Ireland, graduated MD from Edinburgh University in 1786. [GME#19]

WIGHTMAN, ROBERT, from Ireland, graduated MD from Edinburgh University in 1789. [GME#21]

WILKIE, STEWART, soldier of the Rothesay and Caithness Fencibles, married Catherine Hallaran, on 6 September 1798. [Cloyne Cathedral, Co. Cork]

WILLES, JAMEDS, from Ireland, graduated MD from
Edinburgh University in 1802. [GME#33]

WILSON, PETER, Captain of the Royal Marines, Dublin, 10
December 1819. [NAS.B2/2.2.283]

WILSON, THOMAS, from Ireland, graduated MD from
Edinburgh University in 1790. [GME#22]

WOLSELEY, JOHN, from Ireland, graduated MD from
Edinburgh University in 1795. [GME#26]

WOODHOUSE, RICHARD THOMAS, from Ireland,
graduated MD from Edinburgh University in 1822.
[GME#69]

WOODWARD, RICHARD, from Ireland, graduated MD from
Edinburgh University in 1821. [GME#66]

YOUNG, JEAN, relict of William Storrie a butcher in
Carrickfergus, 25 November 1726.
[NAS.B64.1.5/339.2/5]

REFERENCES

Archives

NAS =   National Archives of Scotland

Publications

CEG =   Catalogue of Graduates in the Faculties of Arts, Divinity and Law of the University of Edinburgh, [Edinburgh, 1858]

F =   Fastii Ecclesiae Scoticanae, [Edinburgh, 1915]

FI =   Fastii of the Irish Presbyterian Church

GME =   Graduates in Medicine in the University of Edinburgh, 1705-1866,   [Edinburgh, 1867]

IBR =   Inveraray Burgess Roll

RGG =   Roll of the Graduates of Glasgow University, 1727-1897 W. I. Addison, [Glasgow, 1898]

SA =   Scottish Americanus, W. Brock, [Edinburgh, 1982]

SP =   The Scots Peerage, J B Paul, [Edinburgh, 1904]